THE CROSS STITCHER'S BIBLE

THE CROSS STITCHER'S BIBLE

Jane Greenoff

David & Charles

Contents

×××××

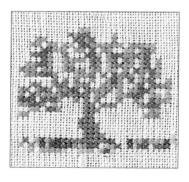

✕✕✕✕✕

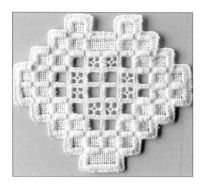

To my husband Bill, whose love makes it all possible!

The Cross Stitch Guild

The Cross Stitch Guild was formed in March 1996 and quickly became a worldwide organisation with a committed and enthusiastic body of members – over 2,000 in the first six months of operation. As word spreads it is clear that many cross stitch and counted thread addicts around the world are delighted to have a Guild of their own. The CSG has received an extraordinary level of support from designers, retailers, manufacturers and stitchers. Guild members receive a full-colour magazine bi-monthly, including free counted cross-stitch designs and technical advice and information.

For more information contact: CSG HQ, Pinks Barn, London Road, Fairford, Gloucestershire GL7 4AR England. Tel: 0800 328 9750.

A DAVID & CHARLES BOOK

First published in the UK in 2000

Text and designs Copyright © Jane Greenoff 2000
Photography and layout Copyright © David & Charles 2000

Stitch Library artworks © David & Charles 2000, adapted from originals supplied by the Cross Stitch Guild

Jane Greenoff has asserted her right to be identified as author of this work in accordance with the Copyright, Designs and Patents Act, 1988.

A catalogue record for this book is available from the British Library.

ISBN 0 7153 0929 3

Photography by Alan Duns and David Johnson
Book design by Casebourne Rose
Printed in China by Hong Kong
Graphics and Printing Ltd
for David & Charles
Brunel House   Newton Abbot   Devon

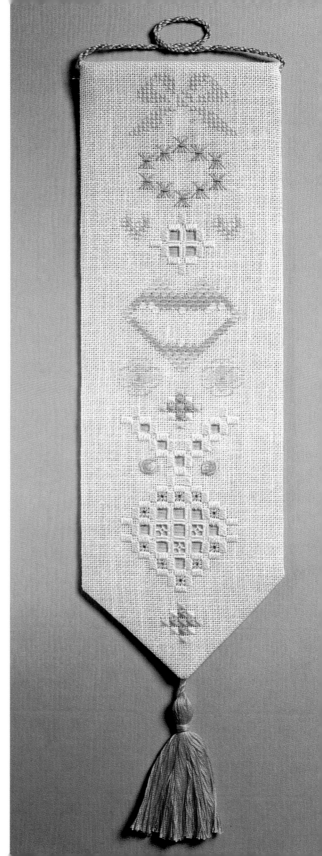

(Page 1)
Poppy and Daisy Posy – see page 15 for instructions.

(Page 2)
Hardanger Flower Chatelaine, Scissors Keeper and Needlecase – see page 74 for instructions.

✳ *Bow Band Sampler* ✳

Stitch Count: 29 x 137
Design Size: 7.5 x 35cm (3 x 14in)
Fabric Selection: Zweigart Cork linen
20 threads to 2.5cm (1in)
Tapestry Needle Size: 24 and 22

This delicate sampler has been stitched in rows using a variety of different stitches, working from top to bottom as follows: cross stitch, half Rhodes stitch with bar, cross stitch with a small Hardanger section, queen stitch, Rhodes stitch, Hardanger with eyelet stitches, Bullion stitch roses and Rhodes stitch. The band sampler is charted on page 164 of the Motif Library. You might find it easier to photocopy the two parts of the chart and tape them together. See Working the Projects page 126.

Introduction

✕✕✕✕✕

I have been asked over and over again 'for a book giving the tips, hints and technical know-how of cross stitch' – and here it is. Pure cross stitch, worked perfectly, is beautiful to look at and simple to do but does require detailed explanations of some of the techniques. So I hope that this unique book will provide the useful, accessible information in an easy-to-use format that so many of you have been seeking.

Cross stitch is usually our first love but I hope that by referring to this book you will be able to add to and enhance your cross stitch patterns and perhaps design for yourself. It is hoped that *The Cross Stitcher's Bible*, with its clear, definitive instructions, computer-generated charts and exciting motif library, will become your essential manual, and that you will not only perfect existing techniques, but also explore exciting companions to cross stitch, such as the use of beads and ribbon, embellishment with charms and buttons, and other decorative counted stitches like blackwork and Hardanger.

✛ How to Use This Book ✛

The book has been divided into sections with colour-coded pages to enable you to find the information you require easily and to provide a clear and comprehensive approach to all aspects of cross stitching.

• Getting Started is colour coded green and tells you all you need to know about choosing and using equipment, fabric and threads plus all the practical aspects of how to cross stitch on Aida and evenweave.

• Creative Options is colour coded yellow and describes cross stitching techniques using some of the many different fabrics and threads available.

• Exploring Choices is colour coded blue and features exciting designs that show you how easy it is to combine cross stitch with many other counted embroidery techniques.

• In Getting Started, Creative Options and Exploring Choices, I have included boxes called Stitch Perfect, which focus on the important points in each section.

• In Creative Options you will see illustrations of worked designs, many of which combine a number of techniques fully explained elsewhere. For example, the Birdhouse (page 54) includes working cross stitch on linen, creating French knots in stranded cotton (floss) and silk ribbon and using a charm for embellishment.

• The extensive Stitch Library includes all the stitches you need to work any of the designs in the book, each with clear, colour diagrams, colour pictures of the completed stitches and explanatory text.

• There is a short section called Working the Projects (page 126). This should be particularly useful for the less experienced stitcher, helping to guide you through the early stages of any project you choose to stitch.

• All of the designs featured in the book are charted in the Motif Library starting on page 127. I have chosen colour charts with black symbols so that you can identify the charts you need but may still photocopy and enlarge them if you wish.

• Most of the designs in the Motif Library may be stitched on Aida or evenweave. Where evenweave is essential it is indicated in the picture caption. All the cross stitch designs have been stitched with DMC stranded cotton (floss) unless otherwise stated.

• Measurements are given in metric with imperial conversions in brackets. Use either metric or imperial when working, do not combine them.

Getting Started

You should find this section very useful as it contains a great deal of invaluable information on cross stitch basics, including how to choose equipment, use charts, manage threads and all the instruction you'll ever need on creating beautiful cross stitch on Aida and evenweave fabric.

×××××

❋ *Yellow Flower* ❋

Stitch Count: 24 x 43
Design Size: 4.5 x 7.5cm (1³/₄ x 3in)
Fabric Selection: Cream Aida 14 blocks to 2.5cm (1in)
Tapestry Needle Size: 24

This simple design has been cross stitched using two strands of stranded cotton (floss). The chart for this design is part of a larger chart in the Motif Library on page 129. See Working the Projects page 126.

Using Charts

The designs are worked from charts and are counted designs. The charts and keys for all the projects are contained in the Motif Library (pages 127–181) and are illustrated in colour with a black and/or white symbol to aid colour identification.

- Each square on a chart, both occupied and unoccupied, represents two threads of linen or one block of Aida unless otherwise stated. Each occupied square equals one stitch.

- The church in winter shown here could have been worked from a black and white chart, a coloured chart or a combination of both, as shown opposite.

- Cross stitch charts generally consist of whole squares representing complete cross stitches, but you will see additional stitches added to some charts in the Motif Library indicating three-quarter cross stitches (sometimes called fractional stitches), French knots and so on. These stitches will be clearly labelled in the key or included on the chart.

- The count of a fabric (the number of stitches to 2.5cm or 1in) affects the size of a finished piece even when worked from the same chart, whether a coloured chart or a black and white one. This is shown clearly on page 16, where a rosebud has been worked on different counts.

- Traditionally cross stitchers begin to stitch from the middle of the chart and the middle of the fabric thus ensuring that the design is centred when it is mounted and framed. To prevent serious counting errors, use a coloured pen to rule a line on the chart from arrow to arrow to find the centre and then add a line of tacking (basting) to the fabric. This can act as an early warning system!

- When looking at a chart, try to plan the direction in which you are going to stitch. If you count across the shortest distances of empty fabric each time you will avoid making counting mistakes. This may sometimes mean that you are counting diagonally, vertically or horizontally across a pattern, which may seem a peculiar route but is one which will actually help prevent counting mistakes. Mistakes most often occur when counting across long sections of blank fabric.

❋ *A Church in Winter* ❋
Stitch Count: 88 x 48
Design Size: 16 x 19cm (6$^1/_2$ x 3$^1/_2$in)
Fabric Selection: Grey Aida 14 blocks to 2.5cm (1in)
Tapestry Needle Size: 24

This winter scene has been stitched using two strands of stranded cotton (floss) for the cross stitch and one strand for the back stitch outlining. It is charted on page 180 of the Motif Library. See Working the Projects page 126.

- You can turn your work and the chart upside down if you prefer to work towards you, but never turn halfway – your stitches will end up facing the wrong way!
- Check your relative position regularly so that you do not belatedly discover mistakes and have lots of stitches to unpick.

- I make a photocopy of a chart from which I am working so that I can lightly colour in the chart as I proceed to avoid looking at the wrong section.
- You may find a metal board with magnetic strips helpful. It keeps the chart in position and marks your place.

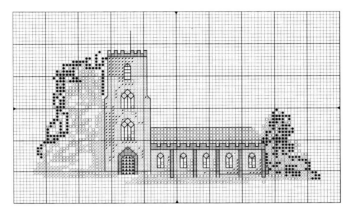

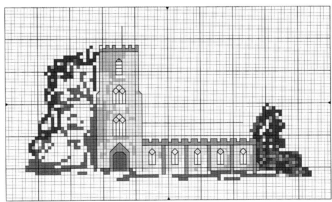

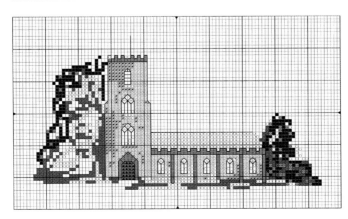

Equipment

The equipment needed for cross stitch couldn't be simpler – essentially just a selection of tapestry needles, some scissors and perhaps a hoop or frame will get you going. You will need other items for making up projects, for example, sewing thread, double-sided adhesive tape, frames, mounts and so on but these will be given under the relevant finishing instructions at the back of the book.

Needles

• When working counted cross stitch you will need blunt tapestry needles of various sizes depending on your fabric selection. A blunt needle is required because you should be *parting* the threads of the fabric rather than piercing the material. You want to avoid splitting the fibres as you stitch.

• The most commonly used tapestry needles for cross stitch are sizes 24 and 26, although needles are available in sizes 20, 22, 24, 26 and 28.

• When using needle sizes 26 and 28, avoid using too many strands of stranded cotton (floss) because the eye is very delicate and will break. Adjust the needle size to match the project. If you are not sure what size of needle to choose, check in the following way: when the needle is pushed through the fabric it should pass through without enlarging the hole, but also without falling through too easily.

• Avoid leaving your needle in the fabric when it is put away as it may leave a mark (unless you are working with gold-plated needles).

• The nickel plating on needles varies and some stitchers find they are allergic to the nickel and therefore prefer gold-plated needles.

• When the use of beads is suggested in a project they may be attached using a special beading needle. A blunt beading needle size 26 has been specially developed for cross stitchers (see Suppliers).

Scissors

• Keep a small, sharp pair of pointed scissors exclusively for your embroidery.

• Use dressmaker's shears for cutting fabric.

Frames and Hoops

• Frames or hoops are not essential for cross stitchers and I have worked without either for many years. I prefer to work my cross stitch in my hand as this allows a sewing action (see Forming a Cross Stitch page 20) but this is a matter of personal preference.

• If you must use a hoop, please use one large enough to hold the complete design – moving a hoop across your beautifully formed stitches is criminal!

• Frames and hoops are useful when you are working in miniature and also when adding beads or combining cross stitch with silk ribbon.

Choosing and Managing Threads

The most commonly used thread for counted embroidery is stranded cotton (floss) but you will see Flower Threads, perlé cottons, assorted metallics and spaced-dyed specialist threads used within the Creative Options section (colour-coded yellow). The following guidelines apply to stranded cotton (floss) as information about other yarns will be found in the relevant sections.

• All the motifs in the Motif Library were stitched using DMC stranded cotton (floss) unless stated otherwise. Anchor alternatives are given in brackets. If you do change to an alternative Anchor number bear in mind that an exact colour match is not always possible.

• Where two shade numbers are quoted for one stitch this is known as tweeding. This straightforward practice is a simple way to increase the numbers of colours in your palate without buying more thread. To tweed, combine more than one coloured thread in the needle at the same time and work as one. You can apply tweeding to working French knots and bullion bars to great effect.

• When selecting threads, always have the fabric

you are intending to use close at hand, because the colour of your background fabric will affect your choice of thread colours. When in a shop, check the colour of the thread in daylight as electric light can 'kill' some shades.

• It is possible to buy 'daylight' bulbs to use in normal spotlights at home – a great help when shading a design in the evening.

• Cross stitch is generally worked using two strands of stranded cotton when working on 14 and 16-count Aida.

• If you are working on Aida and are not sure how many strands to use, try working a small section, stitching a few complete cross stitches and looking at the stitching in daylight. Some colours may need the number of strands adjusting to suit the project.

• If you are working on evenweave and do not know how many strands of stranded cotton (floss) to use, carefully pull a thread from the edge of the fabric and compare the thread with the strands of cotton. The strands on the needle should be a similar weight.

• When using two strands or more for your

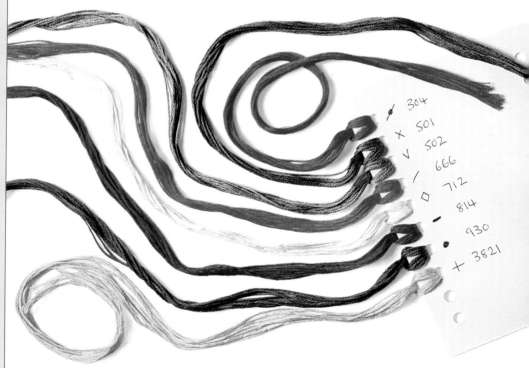

cross stitch, you will need to re-align the strands before starting to stitch. Simply separate the strands and then realign them before threading your needle. When using some fibres it is helpful to pass the threads through a lightly dampened sponge which helps to remove unwanted static from the threads.

• Before laundering or tea-dyeing a piece of work (see page 32) you need to ensure that the threads are colourfast. To do this place the work face down on a clean surface and using a clean, damp white tissue, press the back of the stitches. Any trace of colour on the tissue means the thread colours are not fast, so do not wash or tea-dye. You should have no trouble with reputable brands such as DMC, Anchor and Madeira but take extra care with Christmas reds.

Organising Your Threads

It really does pay to start with good habits if possible and have an organiser system for your threads.

• There are many excellent organiser systems on the market, but I make my own organiser cards as shown in the photograph. The card from inside a packet of tights is excellent, but any stiff card will do.

• Punch holes down each side of the card and take a skein of stranded cotton (floss). Cut the cotton into manageable lengths of about 80cm (30in) double them and thread them through the holes as shown. It is quite simple to remove one length of thread from the card without disturbing the rest.

• If you label the card with the manufacturer's name and shade number, when the project is complete all the threads will be labelled ready for another project.

✳ *Poppy and Daisy Posy* ✳
Stitch Count: 29 x 39
Design Size: 6 x 7.5cm (2$^{1}/_{4}$ x 3in)
Fabric Selection: Zweigart Cashel linen 28 threads to 2.5cm (1in)
Tapestry Needle Size: 24

Two strands of stranded cotton (floss) were used for the cross stitch with one strand of the shade indicated in the chart key to add the optional back stitch outline. It is charted on page 129 of the Motif Library. See Working the Projects page 126.

Starting to Stitch

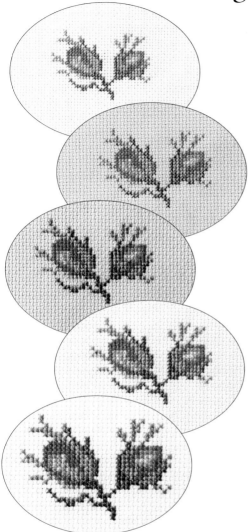

❋ *Pink Rosebuds* ❋
Stitch Count: 33 x 24
Fabric Selection: Aida in five different thread counts 11,
14, 16, 18 and 20 to 2.5cm (1in)
Tapestry Needle Size: 24–26

A simple rosebud has been stitched on different counts of Aida to show how the size of the design is altered by the fabric count and how different coloured fabrics affect the overall look of the design. The cross stitch has been stitched using two strands for the 11, 14 and 16-count fabrics and one strand for the 18 and 20-count materials. The rosebud chart is on page 128 of the Motif Library. See Working the Projects page 126.

This section of the book is intended to create the background for the later sections, Creative Options and Exploring Choices. Whether you are an expert cross stitcher or just beginning, please read through this section in case there are tips and hints you may not have heard before. You may be able to see the reasons for some of the things you do or perhaps the reasons why you should! When working the projects in the book beginners might find the section called Working the Projects on page 126 useful as it provides a checklist to get your project started.

Fabrics for Cross Stitching
The fabric predominantly used for counted needlework is divided into two main groups: Aida – woven in definite blocks, or evenweave – woven in single threads. (Refer also to page 24 Choosing and Using Fabrics.)

Stitching on Aida
All the fabrics in the Aida family are woven with the threads grouped in bundles to form a square pattern on the fabric which in turn creates obvious holes. The stitches are formed using these holes. Aida is available in many different colours and counts. The rosebud motif on this page (charted on page 128 in two colourways) has been stitched on different coloured fabrics with different thread counts. As you can see the colour changes make it look quite different and using various counts results in different sized motifs. To check the thread count, lay a ruler on top of the material and, using a needle, count the number of threads or blocks to 2.5cm (1in).

Stitching on Evenweave
This is the name given to a range of fabrics where the threads are woven singly rather than in blocks. Evenweaves are available in many colours and counts and working on evenweave is not difficult, just different. The designs opposite are the same size on evenweave as on Aida because each stitch is formed over two threads instead of one block, therefore a 28-count evenweave has the same stitch count as a 14-count Aida (28 threads to 2.5cm = 14 blocks to 2.5cm). Evenweave can be worked over one thread (see page 31) or when very fine detail is required. It is also possible to stitch poems or other text

within a small sampler if the border is worked over two threads and the text over one thread.

How Many Strands?

The number of strands of stranded cotton (floss) used depends mainly on the stitch count of the fabric you are using. When in doubt, work a few cross stitches in the fabric margin and decide how many strands you prefer. If the chart you wish to stitch does not indicate how many strands to use, you can check by pulling a thread from the edge of the fabric and comparing it with the strands of cotton. They should be a similar weight to the threads in the fabric.

Calculating Design Size

This is the area that many stitchers avoid if they possibly can, but if you are going to progress from purchased cross stitch kits and move to working from charts or better still, your own designs, you must know how to work out design sizes. It is this calculation which decides how much fabric you will need to stitch your project or whether a particular motif will fit in a card aperture. There is nothing worse than working a project and realising belatedly that the whole design will not fit on the fabric!

All counted designs are made up of squares or parts of squares and the fabrics used for counted cross stitch are produced to have the same number of threads or blocks in each direction so that you will produce nice square stitches. All that determines the size of a cross stitch design is the number stitches up and down and the thread count of the fabric. To calculate the size of a design follow these principles:

• Look at your completed chart and count the number of stitches in each direction.

• Divide this number by the number of stitches to 2.5cm (1in) on the fabric of your choice and this will determine the completed design size. For example, 140 stitches divided by 14-count Aida equals a design size of 10in.

• Always add a margin for stretching, framing or finishing. I always add 13cm (5in) to both dimensions when designing a picture or sampler. This can be reduced to 7.5cm (3in) for smaller projects. Remember when creating a card or trinket pot to allow the margin on the aperture size not the stitch count.

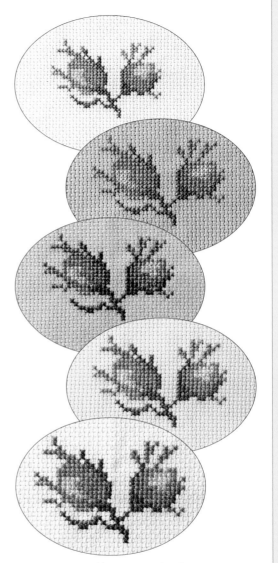

✳ *Yellow Rosebuds* ✳

Stitch Count: 33 x 24

Fabric Selection: Aida in five different thread counts 11, 14, 16, 18 and 20 to 2.5cm (1in)

Tapestry Needle Size: 24–26

Here, the rosebud has been stitched in a yellow colourway, again on different counts of Aida. The cross stitch has been stitched using two strands for the 11, 14 and 16-count fabrics and one strand for the 18 and 20-count materials. The rosebud chart is on page 128 of the Motif Library. See Working the Projects page 126.

Where to Start

Unless indicated otherwise by the designer, start stitching in the middle of a design to ensure an adequate margin for stretching and framing.

- To find the middle of the fabric, fold it in four and press lightly.
- Open out and work a narrow line of tacking (basting) stitches following the threads to mark the fold and the centre. These stitches are removed when the work is completed.
- Rule a line on the chart (if using a copy) to match the tacking (basting) stitches.
- Check you have all the colours you need and mount all the threads on a piece of card alongside its shade number (see page 15).
- Sew a narrow hem or oversew the raw edges to prevent fraying. This can be removed on completion. Avoid sticky tape and any clear glues as they have a habit of creeping and will attract grime to your fabric.
- Work one large cross stitch at the top of your work away from the stitching to remind you which is the top and which way the work is facing.
- If using evenweave, start your stitching to the left of the vertical thread (see Fig 1).

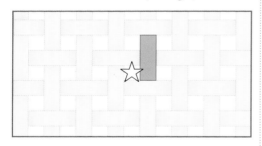

Fig 1 Starting the stitching to the left of a vertical thread

How to Start

It is important to start and finish your stitching neatly, avoiding the use of knots which would create ugly lumps in the finished piece.

Knotless Loop Start

Starting with a knotless loop (fig 2) can be very useful with stranded cotton (floss), but it only works if you are intending to stitch with an *even* number of threads, i.e. 2, 4, or 6.

- Cut the stranded cotton (floss) roughly twice the length you would normally need and carefully separate one strand.
- Double this thread and then thread your needle with the two ends.
- Pierce your fabric from the wrong side where you intend to place your first stitch, leaving the looped end at the rear of the work.
- Return your needle to the wrong side after forming a half cross stitch, and pass the needle through the waiting loop.
- The stitch is now anchored and you may begin to stitch.

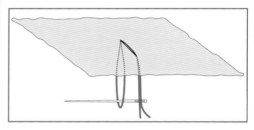

Fig 2 Knotless loop start

Away Waste Knot

Start with an away waste knot (fig 3) if working with an *odd* number of strands or when tweeding threads (where you use one strand each of two or more colours to achieve a mottled, tweedy appearance – see page 14). An away waste knot is situated on the front of the fabric and you work towards it and cut it off when the threads are anchored. Avoid using this method with black thread as it may leave a small shadow on the fabric. (See also Linen Masterclass Stitch Perfect page 22.)

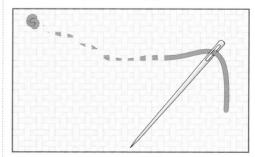

Fig 3 Away waste knot start

Stitch & Park

When working with a number of different shades you can use a number of needles at a time to avoid stopping and starting over again. Work a few stitches in one shade, bring the needle out to the front of the work and park it above where you are stitching. Introduce another colour, work a few stitches and then park before bringing back the previous colour, working under the back of the stitches. Use a gold-plated needle to avoid any risk of the needle marking the fabric.

Working a Cross Stitch

A cross stitch has two parts and can be worked in one of two ways – a complete stitch can be worked, or a number of half stitches may be stitched in one line, then completed on the return journey. Your cross stitch may face either direction but the one essential rule is that *all* the top stitches should face the same direction to produce the neatest result.

✳ *Victorian Flower Garland* ✳

Stitch Count: 40 x 69
Design Size: 7.5 x 12.5cm (3 x 5in)
Fabric Selection: Cream Aida 14 blocks to 2.5cm (1in) or pure antique white linen 28 threads to 2.5cm (1in)
Tapestry Needle Size: 24

These two identical designs have been worked using two strands of stranded cotton (floss) for the cross stitch – one on Aida and one on evenweave so you can compare the results. The chart for this design is on page 129 of the Motif Library. See Working the Projects page 126.

To create perfect cross stitches the strands of thread first need to be aligned. Take two strands of stranded cotton (floss), separate the strands completely and then realign them before threading your needle. When using some fibres it is helpful to pass the threads through a lightly dampened sponge which helps remove unwanted static and make stitching easier.

Forming a Single Cross Stitch on Aida or Evenweave

Bring the needle up from the wrong side of the fabric at the bottom left of an Aida block or to the left of a vertical evenweave thread (see fig 1 page 18). Cross one block of Aida or two threads of evenweave and insert the needle into the top right-hand corner (see figs 4 and 5). Push through and come up at the bottom right-hand corner. Complete the stitch in the top left-hand corner. To work an adjacent stitch, bring the needle up at the bottom right-hand corner of the first stitch.

Forming Cross Stitch in Two Journeys

Work the first leg of the cross stitch as above but instead of completing the stitch, work the next half stitch and continue to the end of the row. Complete the cross stitches on the return journey. I recommend this method as it forms neater vertical lines on the back of the work.

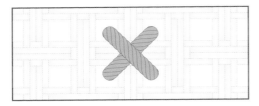

Fig 4 A cross stitch on Aida

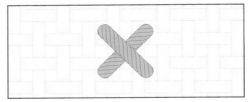

Fig 5 A cross stitch on evenweave

✛ Stitch Perfect ✛

• Use the correct size needle for the fabric and the number of strands of thread required.

• When you start stitching on evenweave fabric, always start to the left of a vertical thread (see fig 1 page 18) as this will help to prevent counting mistakes.

• Start with a knotless loop start or an away waste knot but avoid using a knot on the reverse of the work.

• Work the cross stitch in two journeys (see page 84) forming neat vertical lines on the wrong side of the work. Use a sewing movement, half cross stitch in one direction, covering these original stitches with the second row. This useful and rapid sewing movement is not possible when working with a hoop or frame.

• To prevent the thread twisting when working the cross stitch in two journeys, either turn the work upside down and let the needle spin, or learn to twist the needle as you stitch. Each time you take the needle out of the fabric, give the needle a half turn and the stitches will lie flat.

• The top stitches should all face the same direction.

• Come up through unoccupied holes where possible to help keep your stitches beautifully formed.

• Plan your route around the chart counting over short distances to avoid counting mistakes (see Charts page 10).

• Do not travel across the back of the fabric for more than two stitches as trailing thread will show on the front of the work (see Stitch & Park page 19).

• When finishing off, push the needle under the vertical loops on the back and snip the thread off close to the stitching.

Back Stitch Outlining with Cross Stitch

You will see from the crocus motif right, that additional back stitches are often used to add definition and dimension to a cross stitch project, although this is a matter of personal taste. Try using subtle shades for the back stitch to avoid adding a hard edge to the stitches (see picture page 126). Avoid black for outlining unless needed for wrought iron or similar motifs. (See page 60 for advice on blackwork.)

As a general rule, I use one strand of stranded cotton and a slightly smaller size needle when adding the back stitch outline, using a thread colour that will enhance the design rather than over-power it. Work back stitch over individual blocks on Aida or pairs of threads on evenweave and avoid working long stitches unless it is to illustrate something like cat's whiskers or ships' rigging. The finished effect will be worth it!

How to Change Threads and Finish Off

Changing threads and finishing your work off correctly will pay dividends, creating a neat appearance and a safe piece of stitching that will stand the test of time.

- At the back of the work, pass the needle under several stitches of the same or similar colour and then snip off the loose end close to the stitching (see fig 6). Small loose ends have a nasty habit of pulling through to the right side!
- Finish the stitches in the direction that you are working. To do this, when the thread needs replacing stop stitching and park the needle above the design. Thread a new needle with the replacement thread and form a few stitches. Now un-park the needle and finish the old thread under the new stitches. This will prevent any stitch distortion on the front of the work.

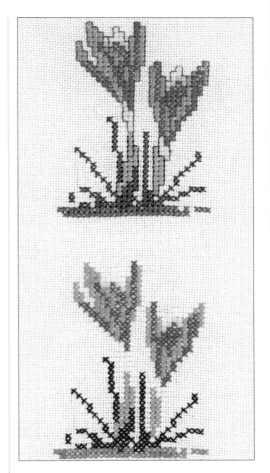

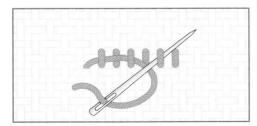

Fig 6 Finishing off a thread

❋ *Purple Crocus* ❋

Stitch Count: 29 x 39
Design Size: 6 x 7.5cm (2¹/₄ x 3in)
Fabric Selection: Cream Jobelan evenweave 27 threads to 2.5cm (1in)
Tapestry Needle Size: 26

This simple but effective crocus motif has been stitched twice, using two techniques but on the same fabric. The top version has been stitched in two strands of stranded cotton (floss) and back stitch outlined in one strand. The outline colour has been taken from the colours used for the cross stitch to ensure a soft, realistic look.

The second version, worked from the same chart (page 152 of the Motif Library), has been stitched using one strand of Flower Thread and the outline has been omitted. You can see that both techniques are effective but give quite a different feel. (See Working the Projects page 126.)

Linen Masterclass

Linen is made from the fibres of the flax plant *Linium usitatissimum*. Unlike other fabrics, linen increases in strength when wet, and it is the perfect choice for cross stitch on table or bed linen and for pulled and drawn thread work.

Linen is an evenweave fabric (see page 16): this means that there are the same number of vertical and horizontal threads to 2.5cm (1in); it does not mean that the threads are all the same thickness or that there will be no slubs or wobbly threads! Unfortunately, these naturally occurring irregularities in the fabric can dissuade some stitchers from using it. Stitching on linen is not difficult, just different: follow my advice and you will discover just how satisfying it is to use.

Railroading

This technique is used to force two strands of stranded cotton (floss) to lie flat and parallel to each other. When pushing the needle through the fabric, pass it in between the two strands of stranded cotton (floss). You can select to railroad both parts of the cross stitch or only the top stitch.

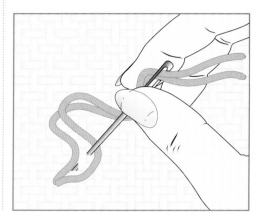

✛ Stitch Perfect ✛

The general instructions for working on evenweave fabrics (see pages 16–21) also apply to linen.

• Use the correct size needle for the fabric (see page 12). To check how many strands of thread you should be stitching with, pull out one thread from the fabric: the thread in your needle should be about the same weight.

• Separate each strand of stranded cotton (floss) and then re-combine ensuring the twist is running in the same direction on each strand.

• To avoid reversing the twist, start stitching with an away waste knot (page 18) rather than the loop method.

• Work cross stitches over two threads in each direction to even out any discrepancies. If more detail is required, stitches can be formed over one thread.

• When stitching over one thread, work the stitches singly rather than in two journeys. This will prevent the stitches sliding under the fabric threads.

• Learn to railroad (see above). Although a time-consuming technique, it does produce effective results. Even simpler, twist the needle as you stitch. As you take the needle out of the fabric, give the needle a half turn: this will keep the thread from twisting and the stitches will lie flat.

• To finish neatly, push the needle under the vertical loops on the back, then snip the thread off close to the stitching.

• When working across the fabric (i.e. on a band sampler), it is good practice to finish the stitches in the direction that you are working. If you run out of thread before the end of the row, see How to Change Threads page 21.

❋ *Lilies* ❋

Stitch Count: 53 x 74
Design Size: 9.5 x 13.25cm (3³/₄ x 5¹/₄in)
Fabric Selection: Unbleached linen 28 threads to 2.5cm (1in)
Tapestry Needle Size: 24–26

These classic lilies are worked on unbleached pure linen using two strands of DMC stranded cotton (floss). The chart for this design is included in the Motif Library (page 137) and could be stitched on any fabric including Aida if preferred. See Working the Projects page 126.

The design has been highlighted with back stitch in one strand of stranded cotton (floss) and the stamen of each lily added with random long stitches.

Creative Options

*T*his section is an invaluable closer look at some of the fabric and thread
options open to the cross stitcher. You will see how easy and rewarding
it is to cross stitch on a variety of materials, including perforated paper, silk,
waste canvas, non-evenweave and double canvas. Some of the many threads
available are explored, showing how effective cross stitching is with yarns other
than stranded cotton (floss), such as Flower Thread, space-dyed thread, rayon,
metallics and blending filaments.

✕✕✕✕✕

Choosing and Using Fabrics

When I first started stitching the choice of fabric
was simple – cream 14-count Aida or linen,
bleached or unbleached! Now there is so much
choice, both in thread count and in colour, so
the only limit is your imagination and your
eyesight! The secret is to select the right fabric
for the project, bearing in mind whether it is
for decoration or a more functional use, and
select a thread count you can manage without
the frustration of working on material which
strains your eyes. Most charted designs will adapt
to suit different fabrics, for example, you can
transfer cross stitch patterns onto canvas and vice
versa. The sunflower design on page 40 has been
stitched on double canvas in wool and again on
unbleached linen in stranded cotton (floss).

The teddy, borage flower, topiary garden, rosebud, poppy and rose shown below have been stitched from the Motif Library on a variety of fabrics using two or three strands of stranded cotton (floss) for the cross stitch. They were stitched over one block of Aida fabrics or over two threads of evenweave fabrics and various needles sizes were used depending on the fabric count. See Working the Projects page 126. Note: Take care with some fabrics as they mark and crease easily, as seen by the embroidery hoop mark still visible on the borage design.

Design	Stitch Count/Design Size	Fabric Selection
Teddy *chart on page 158*	61 x 70 8 x 10cm (3 x 3$\frac{1}{2}$in)	Acrylic Afghan (stitched over one thread)
Borage Flower *chart on page 141*	33 x 28 7.5 x 6.5cm (3 x 2$\frac{1}{2}$in)	Damask with Aida panel 11 blocks to 2.5cm (1in) (stitched over one block)
Topiary Garden *chart on page 141*	48 x 47 9 x 9cm (3$\frac{1}{2}$ x 3$\frac{1}{2}$in)	Antique white linen 28 threads to 2.5cm (1in) (stitched over two threads)
Rosebud *chart on page 141*	24 x 45 4.5 x 8.5cm (1$\frac{3}{4}$ x 3$\frac{1}{4}$in)	Zweigart pure wool Aida 14 blocks to 2.5cm (1in) (stitched over one block)
Purple Pansy *chart on page 151*	29 x 24 5 x 4cm (2 x 1$\frac{1}{2}$in)	Pale green Aida 16 blocks to 2.5cm (1in) (stitched over one block)
Victorian Poppy *chart on page 127*	25 x 26 5 x 5cm (2 x 2in)	Zweigart Cashel unbleached linen 28 threads to 2.5cm (1in) (stitched over two threads)
Cabbage Rose *chart on page 127*	26 x 25 5 x 5cm (2 x 2in)	Yorkshire Aida 14 blocks to 2.5cm (1in) (stitched over one block)

Embroidery Threads

There is now a vast range of thread types available for cross stitch embroidery. Some of the most common are shown here.

Perlé Cotton reel
Glossy, single-ply pure cotton thread often used for Hardanger embroidery

Flower Thread (German) on card or skein
Unmercerised single-ply pure cotton thread with a matt finish

Stranded Cotton (DMC and Anchor)
Six strand mercerised cotton thread, usually divided before use. Supplied as solid or variegated colours

Variegated stranded cotton (DMC & Anchor)
See above

Perlé Cotton skein
Glossy, single-ply pure cotton thread often used for Hardanger embroidery

Caron Collection Watercolours
Space-dyed (hand-painted), pure cotton 3-ply thread. May be divided before use

Caron Collection Waterlilies
Space-dyed (hand-painted), 12-ply pure silk thread. May be divided before use

Appleton Crewel Wool
Fine embroidery wool which may be used singly or combined to suit the ground fabric

Stranded Rayon Thread
Very shiny non-metallic, 4-ply divisible thread ideal used as a contrast with other yarns

Silk Ribbon
Produced specially by YLI for embroiderers, these ribbons may be used like embroidery thread in a needle or may be added to the surface of the project and stitched in position. Commonly used widths are 2mm, 3mm and 4mm.

Cross Stitch on Stitching Paper

Fabric isn't the only material you can cross stitch on. Stitching paper (also called perforated paper) can be stitched, folded, glued and cut to make pretty cross stitch projects and used to fill scrap books and treasure albums. Stitching paper is based on early Victorian punched paper, also referred to as Bristol Board and made in England as early as 1840. The Victorians used it to work bookmarks, needlecases, pincushions, glove and handkerchief boxes, notebook covers and greeting cards. You will see from the photographs here that the style of cross stitch work on paper can look very different. The cut-out of the small Berlin rose posy has a very different feel to the jolly Christmas-style cut-outs and the wild strawberry card. See page 185 for mounting work into cards.

✴ *BerlinRose Posy* ✴
Stitch Count: 30 x 26
Design Size: 6 x 5cm (2¼ x 2in)
Fabric Selection: Stitching paper 14 stitches to 2.5cm 1in
Tapestry Needle Size: 24

Cutting perforated paper after stitching allows you to create a decorative edging, as shown with this Berlin Rose Posy design, where one line of squares outlines the design. The design could then be mounted on a different coloured stitching paper, with further decorative cutting. The posy was cross stitched using three strands of stranded cotton (floss) and is charted on page 139 of the Motif Library.

✛ Stitch Perfect ✛

- Although stitching paper is quite strong, it needs to be handled with care.

- There is a right and a wrong side to the paper, the smoother side being the right side.

- Avoid folding the paper unless this is part of the design.

- Find the centre with a ruler and mark with a pencil. Pencil lines can be removed with a soft rubber.

- Use three strands of stranded cotton (floss) for the cross stitch and two strands for back stitch outlining and lettering.

- Complete all the stitching before starting any cutting.

- Draw the cutting lines on the back of the completed stitching using a soft pencil.

- Use small, sharp-pointed scissors or a good craft knife to cut out the design and any decorative elements of the pattern.

- Stick completed sections together using double-sided adhesive tape.

✴ *Poinsettia Cracker Trim* ✴
Stitch Count: 52 x 15
Design Size: 10 x 2.5cm (4 x 1in)

✴ *Bells Cracker Trim* ✴
Stitch Count: 41 x 22
Design Size: 7.5 x 4cm (3 x 1½in)

These cracker trims (charts on page 139 of the Motif Library) have been worked on stitching paper 14 stitches to 2.5cm (1in) with a size 24 tapestry needle. Three strands of stranded cotton (floss) were used for the cross stitch and two for back stitch. The stitched designs were cut out and fixed to crackers with double-sided tape.

✳ *Strawberry Card* ✳

Stitch Count: 43 x 58
Design Size: 8 x 10cm (3 x 4in) completed card size

✳ *Bible and Cross Card* ✳

Stitch Count: 43 x 58
Design Size: 8 x 10cm (3 x 4in) completed card size

These pretty Victorian-style cards are worked on stitching paper 14 stitches to 2.5cm (1in) with a size 24 tapestry needle. Three strands of stranded cotton (floss) were used for the cross stitch and two for the back stitch detail. The stitched designs were cut out, mounted onto layers of different coloured stitching paper and plain card and fixed together with double-sided tape. The decoration can be embellished by use of careful cutting, as shown in the Berlin Rose Posy opposite. The designs are charted on page 140 of the Motif Library.

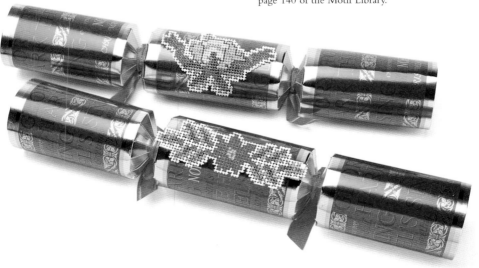

Stitching in Miniature

The photographs here demonstrate at a glance the effect achieved by changing the fabric count used for a project to create not just a smaller version of the design but a different image. The two flower motifs, a rose and pansy (charted in the Motif Library, pages 127 and 151 respectively) have been stitched in miniature using two different stitches to suit the specific fabric. Both flowers have been stitched twice – once in tent stitch on evenweave and once in cross stitch on silk gauze. Both motifs have also been stitched on 'normal' stitch counts – see pages 24/25.

Cross stitchers generally think stitching on silk gauze 40 stitches to 2.5cm (1in) is out of the question because it sounds so fine but it is much less taxing than first imagined. Silk gauze is constructed in such a way that although the stitch count is high, the holes in the fabric are large and are easier to see than you think! The secret is to have the fabric prepared as described below and work in a good light with the correct size gold-plated needle. I use a size 28 needle and work under a standard lamp which gives a wonderful light but doesn't get too hot!

When working on silk gauze you will need to use a simple mount board frame. Cut two pieces of stiff mount board to the size of your fabric. Now cut two sections out of the centre of each piece of board – the cut-out sections need to be just big enough to work the embroidery. Then, using double-sided adhesive tape, sandwich the silk gauze piece between the two boards. The frame can easily be removed once stitching is completed.

✳ *Cabbage Rose* ✳

Stitch Count: 26 x 25
Design Size: Silk gauze 2 x 2cm ($^3/_4$ x $^3/_4$in); linen 2.5 x 2.5cm (1 x 1in)
Fabric Selection: Silk gauze 40 threads to 2.5cm (1in)
or pure linen 28 threads to 2.5cm (1in)
Tapestry Needle Size: 26–28

This tiny rose, made up as a pretty brooch and card, is worked in cross stitch over one thread of the silk gauze or in tent stitch over one thread of linen, using one strand of stranded cotton (floss). It is charted on page 127 of the Motif Library. See Working the Projects page 126 and Mounting Work in Cards page 185.

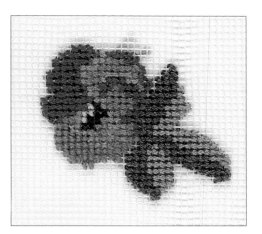 

✳ *Purple Pansy* ✳

Stitch Count: 29 x 24
Design Size: Silk gauze 2 x 2cm (³/₄ x ³/₄in);
linen 2.5 x 2.5cm (1 x 1in)
Fabric Selection: Silk gauze 40 threads to 2.5cm (1in)
or pure linen 28 threads to 2.5cm (1in)
Tapestry Needle Size: 26–28

This tiny pansy has been worked in cross stitch over one thread of silk gauze (shown on the left) and again in tent stitch over one thread of linen (on the right), using one strand of stranded cotton. It is charted on page 151 of the Motif Library. See Working the Projects page 126.

✛ Stitch Perfect ✛
Working on Evenweave in Miniature

• If working cross stitch over one thread on evenweave, work each stitch individually rather than in two journeys to stop the underneath stitches sliding under neighbouring fabric threads.

• If working over one thread on linen (or any evenweave) use tent stitch rather than half cross stitch as tent stitch will give better coverage of the fabric and keep the stitches in position. If half cross stitch is used the threads will slide under neighbouring fabric threads.

• Select fabric with care, with the minimum of slubs and imperfections which are less easily disguised working over one thread.

✛ Stitch Perfect ✛
Working on Silk Gauze in Miniature

• Silk gauze should be worked in a small mount board frame to prevent the fabric distorting (see page 30).

• Silk gauze is constructed in a similar way to interlock canvas, to ensure that the threads will not slide.

• Half cross stitch or full cross stitch may be used successfully.

• Try stitching a small section to check your tension because you may find that half cross stitch is adequate.

• Avoid carrying threads across the back of work because it will show from the front – as you can see!

Stitching on Non-Evenweave

So far we have seen how cross stitching looks on evenweave fabrics but non-evenweave or un-evenweave linen was used to create samplers and counted masterpieces long before the concept of evenweave had been invented, and it is exciting to attempt to recreate a design on non-evenweave material. The traditional Acorn and Flower Sampler shown here has been stitched on linen scrim, a non-evenweave but pure linen fabric which usually ends up as tea-towels or dish-cloths and is not intended for embroidery.

The term 'evenweave' refers to the method used to manufacture the fabrics we use for cross stitch and does not mean that the material will have no lumps and bumps! This misunderstood term means that when the fabric is woven, the number of warp and weft threads (along the length and across the width) are the same. This is why when you work a cross stitch on evenweave fabric, the stitch appears square rather than squashed, shortened or elongated. However, cross stitches worked on non-evenweave fabric *will* be affected by the uneven weave, becoming slightly shortened or elongated, therefore you will need to experiment with the characteristics of the fabric to achieve the best results.

Ageing Linen

It is easy to add the appearance of age to a piece of linen by dipping it in black tea. The fabric to be aged in this way must be a pure, natural fabric such as pure cotton or pure linen. Tea-dyeing can be done on the fabric alone before you start stitching or to the whole piece when the embroidery is completed, though you need to make sure that the threads used are colour-fast (see page 15). After dipping the fabric or needlework in the tea, allow it to dry naturally and then press as normal.

✢ Stitch Perfect ✢

• To know non-evenweave fabric and its foibles, work a square of twenty tacking stitches counting over two threads, and you will see the way in which the fabric creates a landscape (long) or portrait (tall) shape.

• Work a small test piece on the fabric and check you have the effect you require.

• If you are planning a traditional sampler, it is important to select motifs which are of the right style and weight and which will benefit from the effect produced by non-evenweave fabric ie, a rabbit when stitched may look more like a hare!

• Don't be afraid to experiment with different motifs which will alter depending on the fabric direction. Trial and error is the way you will achieve the most successful results.

• You may need to use a loose tension to avoid the threads distorting and giving a pulled thread appearance to the design.

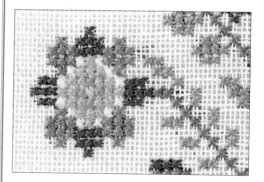

✴ *Acorn and Flower Sampler* ✴

Stitch Count: 81 x 101
Design Size: 17.5 x 21.5cm (7 x 8¹/₂in)
Fabric Selection: Non-evenweave linen 24 threads to 2.5cm (1in)
Tapestry Needle Size: 22

This example of a traditional child's-style sampler was stitched using three strands of stranded cottons (floss) for the cross stitch. The design assumes a slightly different shape as the fabric is not evenweave. The design is charted on page 130/131 of the Motif Library. Use the alphabet charted on page 142 to stitch your own initials (or use any suitable alphabet from the Motif Library). See Working the Projects page 126.

Using Waste Canvas

Waste canvas is a really useful material which enables the cross stitcher to transfer charted designs on to fabrics which were not intended for that purpose and therefore do not have an even, countable weave. Today, the most commonly used application for this technique is to add designs to sweat shirts, T-shirts and baby clothes.

Waste canvas is a comparatively new product although the technique has been used for many years but with linen as the 'waste' fabric. Waste canvas is a double canvas treated with a water-soluble starch product which makes it simple to remove the threads after stitching, but is quite unsuitable for any other type of use. It is easily distinguished by the blue line running through the fabric. The waste material is applied to the garment or fabric and the grid is used to count whilst the design is stitched and then the threads of the canvas are removed. As you can see by the photographs here, the technique is worked in three stages and is described fully in Stitch Perfect.

1   Tack the waste fabric in position.
2   Stitch the design from the chart.
3   Remove the waste threads.

Once all the waste threads have been removed, check for any missed stitches and add any additional back stitch outlining that might be needed to complete the design. Press the finished piece of stitching from the wrong side on soft towels (see page 182).

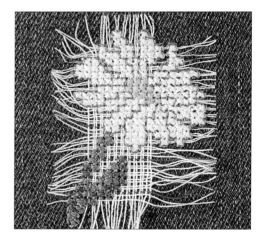

✳ *Single Daisy* ✳

Stitch Count: 19 x 30
Design Size: 4 x 5cm (1¹/₂ x 2¹/₄in)
Fabric Selection: Waste canvas 14 blocks to 2.5cm (1in) on to a piece of blue denim
Tapestry Needle Size: 24

These pictures show the three stages for stitching with waste canvas. The daisy was stitched using two strands of stranded cotton (floss) working each stitch individually through the grid of the waste canvas and the ground fabric. The first stage shows the design stitched on the waste canvas. The second stage shows the waste canvas threads being removed and the third stage reveals the daisy on the denim. The design is charted on page 156 of the Motif Library. See Working the Projects page 126.

✳ *Ox-eye Daisy* ✳ *and Poppy Spray*

Stitch Count: 39 x 57
Design Size: 7.5 x 10cm (3 x 4in)
Fabric Selection: Waste canvas 14 blocks to 2.5cm (1in) on to a piece of blue denim
Tapestry Needle Size: 24

This design was stitched using two strands of stranded cotton (floss) working each stitch individually through the grid of the waste canvas and the ground fabric. The design is charted on page 157 of the Motif Library. See Working the Projects page 126.

✛ Stitch Perfect ✛

• Select the correct stitch count waste fabric for the design and if unsure, work a small test piece confirming the number of strands of stranded cotton (floss) required.

• Use the best quality thread (e.g. DMC, Anchor or Madeira) to avoid colour runs.

• Cut waste canvas at least 5cm (2in) larger than the completed design size.

• Tack the waste fabric in position carefully, as it must stay put whilst you work, using horizontal and vertical tacking lines.

• Work the cross stitch design from a chart, working each stitch individually though the grid of the canvas and the ground fabric.

• When working on a large count waste material, work through the small holes on the canvas as this will keep the stitches

firmly in position and prevents variable tension.

• When the stitching is complete, trim away any excess waste canvas and lightly spray with cold water. This releases the starch and makes removing the threads easier, but rather sticky, so wash your hands regularly or better still use tweezers.

• Pull out the threads one at a time, varying the direction from which you are working to avoid any distortion.

• When all the waste canvas has been removed check for missed stitches which may be added carefully with a sharp needle.

• If using this technique on clothing (like the denim in the photographs) wash on the normal wash cycle for the garment but press the stitched section on the wrong side where possible.

Three-Dimensional Cross Stitch

Working counted cross stitch is very satisfying although it is sometimes described as working in a single dimension and critics of the craft think that the finished work is rather flat! We believe that this is ill-informed but what better way of proving this than asking Meg Evershed of the Nutmeg Company to design a three-dimensional piece for this book. Meg is a UK designer, well known for her three-dimensional embroidery. She uses traditional cross stitch fabrics like Aida and evenweave but also uses plastic canvas in ready-cut shapes as templates to support her designs. The plastic canvas is not used for the stitching. Her beautiful Carousel Trinket Box illustrated here is a perfect demonstration of the versatility of cross stitch. The measurements for making the box are given in metric only for accuracy.

There are three stages in making a three-dimensional cross stitch piece:

Stitching – working the cross stitch design on the fabric from a cross stitch chart.

Mounting – attaching the fabric to plastic canvas pieces cut to a given size and shape.

Assembly – stitching the pieces together to form the finished design.

✳ *The Carousel Trinket Box* ✳

Stitch Count: see charts on pages 132/133 of the Motif Library
Fabric Selection: Antique white Aida 18 blocks to 2.5cm (1in)
Tapestry Needle Size: 24

You Will Need
39 x 11cm 18-count Aida in antique white
30 x 23cm 28-count evenweave in ivory
7.5cm diameter circle of wadding (batting)
Two 7.5cm diameter plastic canvas circles
25 x 9cm 7-mesh plastic canvas
DMC stranded cotton as listed in the chart key on pages 132/133
Matching sewing thread
Size 26 tapestry needle and a sewing needle
Embroidery frame if required

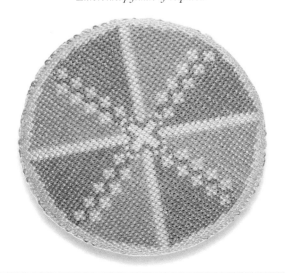

✛ Stitch Perfect ✛

• Before you begin to cross stitch the carousel trinket box, cut the side, inner edge and lid rim from the plastic canvas. Roll them up together and place a rubber band around them to encourage them to assume a circular shape.

• Be careful when stitching the top of the box. It's very easy to lose your sense of direction working a circular design so that the top strokes of the stitches end up lying in different directions. It will help if you mark the top edge of the design.

• The 'stitch & park' technique (see page 19) is very useful for all the different shaded colours on the ponies.

• Make sure you have completed all the cross stitch before you begin the back stitch, referring to the chart on pages 132/133 for shade numbers.

Stitching

1 Work the top, rim and sides for the trinket box on 18-count Aida from the design given in the Motif Library on pages 132/133. Note that the charts for the rim and sides must be repeated twice to give the full length.

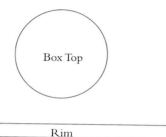

Fig 1

2 Position the designs on the fabric with a margin of at least 1cm around them on all sides. Mark the areas to be stitched on the fabric using tacking (basting) stitches (remembering that the rim and sides are worked twice).

3 Work all the cross stitch, back stitch and the French knots for the ponies' noses using one strand of thread only. Complete all the cross stitch before you begin the back stitch. This is worked only on the ponies and their poles, and all the back stitching on the poles is worked using DMC stranded cotton (floss) 413.

For all the ponies, back stitch the eyes and mouths using DMC 413. Work French knots for the nostrils with one strand of thread, keeping them as small as possible.

On the blue ponies, outline their heads using DMC 341. Work the back stitch outlining the chests and legs using DMC 340, and all the remaining back stitch using DMC 3746.

On the pink ponies, back stitch around the heads using DMC 3609. Work the outlining for the chests and legs using DMC 3608, and all the remaining back stitch on these ponies using DMC 3607. Remove the outlining tacking stitches when you have completed the embroidery.

Mounting

1 From a sheet of 7-mesh plastic canvas, cut the plastic pieces for the box side, inner edge and lid rim. The rim should measure 24 x 1.7cm (on 7-mesh canvas this will be 63 holes x 3 holes); the sides should measure 24 x 2.8cm (63 holes x 7 holes) and the inner edge should measure 22.6 x 3.2cm (58 holes x 8 holes). The sides of the box are mounted on these cut pieces, and the lid and base are each mounted on a plastic canvas circle.

2 For the top of the trinket box, cover one of the plastic circles with wadding (batting), over-sewing around the outside edge. Carefully cut the cross stitched top from the Aida fabric, leaving a margin of at least 1cm all round the embroidery. Run a gathering thread around the outside edge of the Aida and lay the wadding-covered circle on the wrong side of the embroidery, with the wadding (batting) against the stitching. Pull up the gathering thread so that the cross stitched design fits over the plastic circle. Fasten off, and work lacing stitches across the back of the circle to ensure that the Aida is firmly attached to the plastic (see fig 2). Cut a circle of evenweave 7.5cm in diameter and sew or stick it to the underside of the box top.

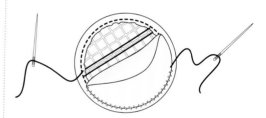

Fig 2

3 For the base of the box, cover the remaining plastic circle with evenweave in the same way as for the top but omit the wadding (batting). Sew or stick another circle of evenweave to the inside of the base.

4 Separate the cross stitched side and lid rim, leaving a margin of at least 1cm around each piece on all sides. Lay the plastic canvas pieces on the wrong side of the stitching, turn in the fabric margins and lace the fabric to the plastic canvas with sewing thread.

5 For the rim, cut a piece of evenweave 25.5

x 3cm and press a narrow seam allowance on all sides with an iron. Sew this to the inside of the rim, so the lacing stitches are covered (fig 3).

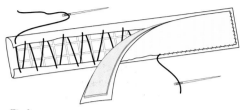

Fig 3

6 For the inner edge, cut a piece of evenweave 24.5 x 8.5cm and press a narrow seam allowance on all sides. Fold the fabric in half, wrong sides facing and long edges together, and press again. Enclose the plastic strip for the inner edge in the fabric, oversewing the edges together (fig 4).

Fig 4

Assembly

1 Join the short edges of the rim, sides and inner edge to produce three circles. Stitch the top edge of the rim around the prepared box top to complete the lid.

2 Put the sides over the inner edge, making sure the joins are at different points. Slip stitch them together keeping the bottom of the inner edge about 2mm above the bottom of the sides. Now stitch the sides to the prepared base (see fig 5). This completes the box. Fit the lid over the inner edge, matching the ponies' poles to give the appearance of a carousel.

Fig 5

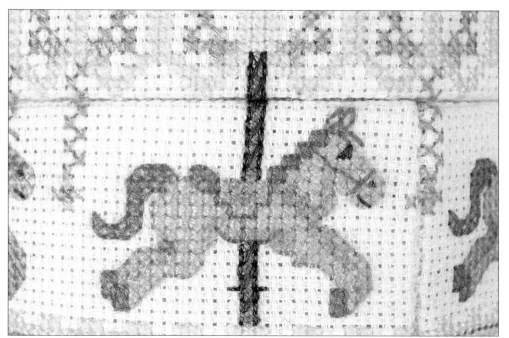

Comparing Double Canvas and Evenweave

Cross stitch charts may be used to work designs on canvas and vice versa, as you can see demonstrated in the photographs below. The sunflower design has been stitched once on linen in stranded cotton (floss) and once on double canvas in Appleton crewel wool. The pansy design has also been stitched twice – once made up into a scissors keeper and worked in beads and stranded cottons on double canvas, with Appleton crewel wool for the background in a colour of your choice. The design was stitched again, this time on linen using stranded cotton (floss) and beads with a simple border worked in a single strand of cotton using four-sided stitch.

The choice of fabric will depend on the stitches used, your eyesight and whether the project is decorative or functional (eg, cushions, chair seats etc.). Canvas is most commonly available in four mesh sizes – 10, 12, 14 and 18-count (threads to 2.5cm/1in). Any gauge of canvas can be used with any chart. Canvas is available in two main types: double-thread (duo) canvas and single-thread (mono) canvas. Refer also to page 42 for working on single canvas.

Double-thread/Duo/Penelope Canvas

This type of canvas is the same as mono canvas except that the threads are grouped in twos in each direction and are usually finer. As with an evenweave fabric, stitches are worked over the

✳ *Sunflower* ✳
Stitch Count: 54 x 72
Design Size: Linen 10 x 13cm (4 x 5¹⁄₄in);
canvas 11.5 x 15cm (4¹⁄₂ x 6in)
Fabric Selection: Zweigart Cashel unbleached linen 28 threads to 2.5cm (1in) or double canvas 12 blocks to 2.5cm (1in)
Tapestry Needle Size: 24–22

This sunflower has been cross stitched once on linen worked over two threads using two strands of stranded cotton (floss) and adding back stitch in one strand. The second version uses Appleton crewel wool on double canvas over two threads, with the centre worked over one thread for more detail. The chart is on page 144 of the Motif Library. The bee motif may be omitted if you prefer. See Working the Projects page 126.

✳ *Beaded Pansy Scissors Keeper* ✳ *& Beaded Pansy Picture*

Stitch Count: 27 x 25 (pansy only)
Design Size: Linen 5 x 5cm (2 x 2in);
canvas 6 x 6cm (2¹/₄ x 2¹/₄in)
Fabric Selection: Picture on ivory linen 28 threads to
2.5cm (1in) and the scissors keeper on double canvas
12 blocks to 2.5cm (1in)
Tapestry Needle Size: 24–22

double threads but if you want to put more detail into part of a design, you can make four times as many stitches by using every canvas thread (see the centre of the canvaswork sunflower opposite). Half cross stitch, full cross stitch and tent stitch may be worked on double canvas.

Designed by Sue Hawkins, Technical Director of the Cross Stitch Guild, both of these pieces are stitched in stranded cotton with the background in Appleton crewel wool. The pansy is charted on page 153 of the Motif Library. The beads used were from Beadesign (see Suppliers). See Working the Projects page 126.

✛ Stitch Perfect ✛

• Before stitching, use a thick tapestry needle to push apart the double threads. This is known as pricking out the canvas and will make stitching easier if you intend to combine working one and two threads.

• When adding beads to a design, using double canvas creates the most satisfactory results as the beads stay in position, not wobbling as they do on single canvas.

• When counting canvas, always count the threads and not the holes, because your stitches are made over threads and not in holes. This is a common stumbling block but you will always get it right if you remember that holes cannot be counted because they are empty and therefore do not exist!

• It is a good idea to bind the edge of your canvas with masking tape before you begin to stitch as this will protect your hands and prevent the yarn repeatedly catching on the cut edge. Ideally this masking tape edge is cut off before you stretch the finished piece.

• A frame is not essential when working on double canvas but is useful if you are using tent stitch.

Working on Single Canvas

I enjoy the contrast of working cross stitch designs on single canvas for a change of effect and I have designed projects commercially using canvas as an alternative to Aida or evenweave. Stitchers are sometimes nervous of transferring designs on to canvas when they were designed for fabric but the principles are the same. Early French samplers were generally stitched on canvas with the background left unstitched with great effect, so have a go. Just remember to count the thread of the canvas and not the holes!

The Knot Garden Pincushion shown here was inspired by the talented UK embroiderer and teacher, Mary Jenkins and has been stitched on single canvas using space-dyed threads and DMC stranded cotton (floss). The knot garden uses double cross stitch, long-legged cross stitch, tent stitch, large cross stitch, queen stitch and French knots – all to great effect. This type of cross stitch design is great fun to work because the framework of the pattern (the dark green hedges and border) is counted but then you can fill sections without looking at the chart all the time! (See page 50 for tips on working with space-dyed threads.)

Single-thread/Mono Canvas

This canvas is constructed of a simple, even weave and is also available in a deluxe quality where the threads are polished before the canvas is woven and so the yarn passes smoothly through the canvas as you stitch. Deluxe is always worth the extra expense to prevent snarling the yarn. This type of canvas is suitable for any piece of work but especially upholstery, such as seat covers where the embroidery will be stretched unevenly when the seat is sat on. The canvas threads are free to move a little on each other and so adjust to the stress rather than tearing. You will find both ordinary and deluxe canvas in white or brown (the latter is known as antique) and you should choose according to the colours of yarn that you will be using.

Interlock Canvas

Single/Mono canvas is also available as interlock canvas. In this type of canvas the threads along the length are in fact double threads, twisted together to hold the cross threads firmly in place. This produces a more stable canvas, ideal for designs which include long stitches, which might otherwise pull loose canvas threads together and so make holes in your work. The disadvantage of interlock canvas is that it is only available in white so you must take care not to stitch too tightly or the white will show through the work. Interlock is very easy to make up once the embroidery is finished because it does not fray at all, unlike mono deluxe canvas which will very quickly fray right to the edge of the stitching unless great care is taken.

✛ Stitch Perfect ✛

• When stitching on mono canvas (ie, single), half cross stitch is not suitable. Refer to the tent stitch photographs on page 95 of the Stitch Library to see the different effects created by half cross stitch and tent stitch.

• If you use half cross stitch on single canvas some of them may actually slip under the weave of the canvas and then they will be very uneven. On single canvas it is best to use continental or diagonal tent stitch (see Stitching in Miniature for working over one thread on linen page 31).

• A word of warning: some commercial kits tell you to work half cross stitch on single canvas. A much better result can be obtained by using tent stitch, but you will probably run out of wool as tent stitch uses about half as much yarn again as half cross stitch. You have to decide whether to purchase more wool or settle for a rather thin-looking finished piece with inferior wearing qualities.

This little sampler is worked in tent stitch with stranded cottons (floss) and a background of Appleton wools, and uses elements from the Motif Library. You can see why canvas projects need to be finished as described on page 183, to remove the distortion that can occur during tent stitching

✳ *Knot Garden Pincushion* ✳

Stitch Count: 63 x 62
Design Size: 11.5 x 11.5cm (4¹/₂ x 4¹/₂in)
Fabric Selection: Single canvas 14 threads to 2.5cm (1in)
Tapestry Needle Size: 22

This design has been worked using a combination of counted stitches with stranded cotton (floss) and space-dyed Caron Watercolours thread. The simplest way to work this project is to create the circular hedges as shown on the chart on page 150 of the Motif Library and then fill with colours and stitches suggested on the chart, or stitches of your own choice. See Working the Projects page 126.

Combining Flower Thread and Stranded Cotton

One of the joys of working cross stitch is that the stitch stays the same throughout the project but the effect can be changed by clever use of different fibres. The effect achieved can be demonstrated by looking at the two violet designs illustrated below. These delicate little flowers have been stitched using two different yarns – stranded cotton (floss) and German Flower Thread.

Stranded cotton is mercerised when manufactured to add a silk-like sheen and is supplied in divisible lengths, whereas Flower Thread is not mercerised and is single-ply, with a matt finish. The soft effect created by this thread is ideal for small flower motifs, and you might try it on the crocus or daisy designs in the Motif Library on pages 152 and 156.

The contrast of thread types can also be clearly illustrated by looking at the Antique Flower Scissors Keeper and Pincushion shown opposite, where the threads used include Flower Thread, stranded cotton (floss) and rayon threads. The pincushion has been cleverly joined together using counted chain stitch which I have whipped using one strand of rayon so that you can see the join! The scissors keeper is also illustrated un-made up so that you can see how it has been constructed.

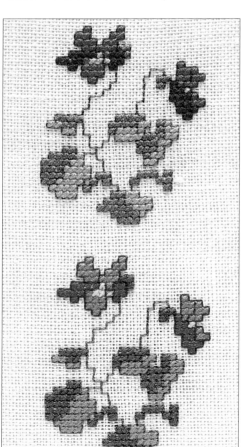

✛ Stitch Perfect ✛

• Experiment with the thread thickness of Flower Thread as it varies slightly.

• Use the correct number of strands for the fabric in question.

• Avoid using Flower Thread for back stitch as it never looks as good as when stitched in one strand of stranded cotton (floss).

• Use shorter lengths of Flower Thread as it becomes rather fluffy if pulled through the fabric too many times.

❋ *Wild Violets* ❋

Stitch Count: 24 x 31
Design Size: 4.5 x 6cm (1³/₄ x 2¹/₄in)
Fabric Selection: Zweigart Cashel cream linen
28 threads to 2.5cm (1in)
Tapestry Needle Size: 24

These delicate little flowers have been stitched over two threads of linen, using two different yarns: the top version in two strands of stranded cotton (floss) and the bottom one in one strand of Flower Thread. The back stitch outline was added using one strand of stranded cotton (floss) on both flowers. The chart is on page 128 of the Motif Library. See Working the Projects page 126.

✳ *Antique Flower* ✳ *Scissors Keeper*

Stitch Count: 22 x 22 (front section only)
Design Size: 4.5 x 4.5cm ($1^3/4$ x $1^3/4$in)
Fabric Selection: Unbleached linen 28 threads to 2.5cm (1in)
Tapestry Needle Size: 24–26

This antique flower design made up as a scissors keeper has been worked over two threads of linen in a mixture of Flower Thread, stranded cotton (floss) and rayon, using one strand of Flower Thread and two strands of cotton and rayon. The scissors keeper is also illustrated un-made up (below) to show the two sections worked with a line of counted chain stitch stitched in preparation for joining at the sides. The chart is on page 163 of the Motif Library. See Working the Projects page 126.

✳ *Antique Flower Pincushion* ✳

Stitch Count: 33 x 33
Design Size: 6.5 x 6.5cm ($2^1/2$ x $2^1/2$in)
Fabric Selection: Unbleached linen 28 threads to 2.5cm (1in)
Tapestry Needle Size: 24–26

The pincushion (above) has been worked over two threads of linen using a mixture of Flower Thread, stranded cotton (floss) and rayon, using one strand of Flower Thread and two strands of cotton and rayon. The completed project was made up using counted chain stitch whipped together. I have used non-matching thread so that you can see the detail on the sides. Normally this thread would match and not be visible. The chart is on page 163 of the Motif Library. See Working the Projects page 126.

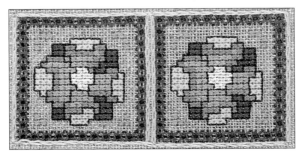

Using Metallic Threads and Blending Filaments

There are now dozens of wonderful vibrant metallic, sparkly and glow-in-the-dark threads available to the cross stitcher. The Christmas tree (right) has been stitched using some rayon thread combined with some of the exciting stranded metallic threads now available. Although metallic threads have been generally regarded as the most difficult to use, the tips included here are from Kreinik who produce the largest range of metallic and blending filaments – so they should help!

I think the secret of using metallic threads is to find the style and thickness needed for the project by looking at the threads when you make your selection. Some fine yarns are referred to as 'braids' but look like normal thread so it is much easier to select by eye unless you have a specific requirement list from the designer. Some yarns are stitched using a needle and some are added to the surface of the design and then stitched in place, so be prepared to experiment. (Silk ribbon and fine lace may also be treated in this way.) When using very glossy metallic gold or silver threads, it is vital that you work with short lengths and a needle large enough help the threads through the fabric. If you work with long lengths you will find that the gold or silver flakes away from the core thread as you work and you lose the metallic effect.

✛ Stitch Perfect ✛

• When using metallic threads and blending filaments stitch more slowly and more attentively, and use a needle large enough to 'open' the hole in the fabric sufficiently to allow the thread to go through easily.

• Use short lengths of thread 46cm (18in) or less to avoid excessive abrasion when pulling the thread through the fabric.

• Let your needle hang frequently (after one or two stitches) so that the thread can untwist.

• Stitch using the 'stab' method rather than the 'hand sewing' method, working your stitches in two movements – up vertically, then down vertically through the fabric.

• To vary the amount of shine, change the number of strands of metallic thread – more strands give a greater sheen, and vice versa.

❋ *Christmas Tree* ❋

Stitch Count: 39 x 53
Design Size: 7.5 x 10cm (3 x 4in)
Fabric Selection: Cream Aida 14 blocks to 2.5cm (1in)
Tapestry Needle Size: 24

This decorative Christmas card has been worked using a variety of stranded metallic threads combined with stranded cotton (floss). The chart is on page 151 of the Motif Library. See Working the Projects page 126.

There are many metallics available and an assortment is shown here.

Blending Filaments

Blending Filaments are light, delicate threads intended to be combined with other fibres, usually with stranded cotton (floss) to add a glisten or sparkle. For example, pearl blending filament is ideal combined with white stranded cotton to create snow effects, as you can see in this pretty snow scene that has been made up into a card.

When combining Blending Filament with stranded cotton (floss) in one needle, you must first knot the metallic thread onto the needle as follows. Loop the thread and pass the loop through the eye of the needle, leaving a short tail. Pull the loop over the point of the needle and tighten the loop at the end of the eye by pulling the two ends of the thread. Gently stroke the knotted thread to 'lock' it in place. Add the stranded cotton by threading onto the needle in the usual way, and you are ready to start stitching.

❄ *Snow Scene* ❄
Stitch Count: 117 x 57
Design Size: 21.25 x 10.25cm (8¹/₄ x 4in)
Fabric Selection: Unbleached Zweigart linen 28 threads to 2.5cm (1in)
Tapestry Needle Size: 24

This chilly winter scene above has been given that extra something by adding pearl blending filament to the snow. The design has been stitched in stranded cottons (floss) but with the blending filament added to all the white used in the project. The chart is on page 178/179 of the Motif Library. See Working the Projects page 126.

❄ *Celebrations* ❄
Stitch Count: 54 x 41
Design Size: 10 x 7.5cm (4 x 3in)
Fabric Selection: Pure linen 28 threads to 2.5cm (1in)
Tapestry Needle Size: 24

This card design, right, which includes three celebration motifs, has been stitched twice, once in stranded cotton (floss) and once using the same stranded colours but with added blending filament. As you can see, the design was pretty when stitched in the normal way but extraordinary with the sparkle added. The chart is on page 181 of the Motif Library. See Working the Projects page 126.

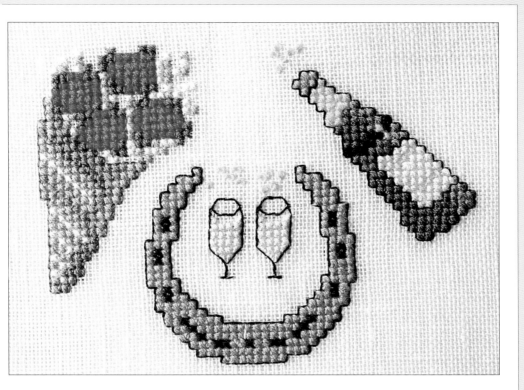

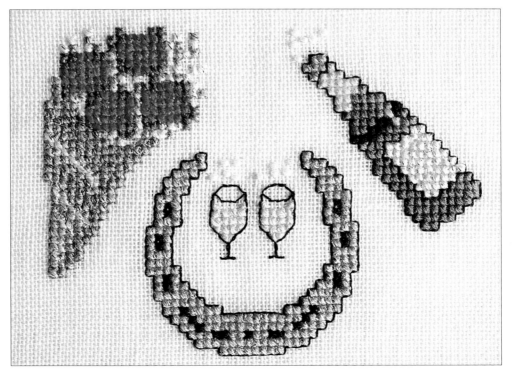

Using Space-Dyed Threads

This section of the book shows you how to create a piece of stitching following a chart in the usual way but with an end result that looks quite different from any one else's version. It is a type of designing without the angst! There are dozens of manufacturers of specialist space-dyed fibres so feel free to experiment. If you cannot find the exact version used in my stitched piece try something else. Space-dyed threads are not random dyed but have shades and patterns of colour making it possible for you to decide where you want a particular shade. Follow the basic guidelines for using space-dyed threads and the effects will surprise you.

You can see from the photograph opposite that the hemmed bookmark has been stitched using stranded cottons (floss) effectively but it has also been stitched using Caron Collection Waterlilies to produce a very different look. It is a very relaxing way to stitch as the whole project is worked from the same skein. The knot garden pincushion shown on page 43 and the autumn panel below (and which also features some Hardanger work), have been stitched using a single strand of space-dyed thread (Caron Watercolours). The Hardanger flower chatelaine shown on pages 2 and 75 also uses some space-dyed threads.

You may like to use variegated threads to introduce a different look to your work. Variegated threads are completely randomly dyed so choosing different sections of colour and predicting how they will change as the thread is used is not possible as it is with space-dyed threads but variegated threads can be useful for working greenery, brick walls and so on.

❊ *Autumn Jewel Panel* ❊
Stitch Count: 60 x 60
Design Size: 12.5 x 12.5cm (5 x 5in)
Fabric Selection: Zweigart Dublin linen 25 threads to 2.5cm (1in)
Tapestry Needle Size: 24–22

This pretty tile is worked in two strands of stranded cottons and one strand of Caron Watercolours thread 062 and includes a little simple Hardanger, Queen stitch, Rhodes stitch, half Rhodes stitch and Algerian eye. The chart is on page 165 of the Motif Library. See Working the Projects page 126. Refer also to the Stitch Library starting on page 83 and Hardanger Embroidery page 70.

✣ Stitch Perfect ✣

• When combining stranded cottons (floss) with space-dyed threads, compare the colours carefully along the length of the thread to check that the shades tone successfully.

• Look at the skein and cut the thread so you can see where colours start and finish.

• Irrespective of the number of strands used for the project, always start with an away waste knot and not the loop start, as the colour order will be disrupted.

• When threading the needle, check the colour you intend to use is near the away waste knot.

• When working cross stitches always complete each cross as you go and do not form cross stitches in two journeys.

• Use a length of thread *only* whilst the colours suit the project. Do not attempt to use the whole length of thread if the colour of that section is not appropriate.

❋ *Hemmed Bookmarks* ❋

Stitch Count: 32 x 79
Design Size: 6.5 x 14.5cm (2^1/$_2$ x 5^3/$_4$in)
Fabric Selection: Pure linen 28 threads to 2.5cm (1in)
Tapestry Needle Size: 26

The design for these delicate self-hemmed bookmarks has been stitched twice – once in stranded cotton (floss) (left) and then in Caron Collection Waterlilies thread (093) (right). You can see how effective the Caron thread is at producing a multi-coloured design from a single skein. Both bookmarks have been finished with four-sided stitch and single or double hem stitching. The narrow ends have been frayed and the design cut out to the hem stitching. The chart is on page 148 of the Motif Library. See Working the Projects page 126.

Exploring Choices

*T**his section features a range of exciting designs showing how easy it is to combine cross stitch with many other counted embroidery techniques. You will discover how much fun it is to bring a whole new dimension to your embroidery with the addition of buttons, charms, beads and ribbon, and how simple it is to enhance your cross stitch with other techniques such as pulled work, drawn thread work, Hardanger, blackwork and hem stitching. There is also invaluable advice on adapting kits and designing your own work.*

Using Charms, Buttons and Embellishments

Charms, buttons and other embellishments may be added to a completed piece of stitching to great effect, although there are pitfalls to avoid. You will need to ensure that the charm size is correct for the project, for example, the animal buttons on the Ark pictured right are the correct scale for the border, just as the bee is the perfect size for the beehive design on page 55.

When selecting metal charms for a completed piece of stitching, avoid cheap, stamped versions as your work deserves the best. Brass charms are manufactured using strong processes and there will be chemical residues left on a charm if it has not been 'finished'. A process of 'dip, tub and roll' is the scouring method used to clean charms for use on embroidery, which prevents potential damage. If a completed piece of stitching is exposed to a damp atmosphere, a chemical reaction may be set up and the fabric could become discoloured. It is possible for blue fabric to have an orange patch where the charm has been in contact with the fabric.

⁕ The Ark and its Creatures ⁕

Stitch Count: 80 x 80
Design Size: 14.5 x 14.5cm (5³/₄ x 5³/₄in)
Fabric Selection: Zweigart Yorkshire Aida 14 blocks to
2.5cm (1in)
Tapestry Needle Size: 24

This charming quilt-style sampler was stitched using two
strands of stranded cotton (floss) for the cross stitch over
one block of Aida and one strand for the back stitch outline.
The decorative porcelain buttons were added with two
strands of matching thread. The chart is on page 155 of the
Motif Library. See Working the Projects page 126.

❋ Birdhouse ❋

Stitch Count: 58 x 39
Design Size: 11 x 7.5cm (4¼ x 3in)
Fabric Selection: Half-bleached linen 28 threads to 2.5cm (1in)
Tapestry Needle Size: 24–26

This nostalgic little picture was stitched over two threads using two strands of stranded cotton (floss) for the cross stitch and one strand for the back stitch. French knots were added in 2mm silk ribbon made by YLI (see Suppliers) and/or one strand of stranded cotton (floss). A brass butterfly charm (see Suppliers) was attached with matching thread. The chart is on page 145 of the Motif Library. See Working the Projects page 126.

There is an increasing array of buttons available, in the craft shops and through mail order. Both decorative buttons (as used on The Ark

and its Creatures) and simple mother-of-pearl or shell buttons may be added to cross stitch to great effect and may also be combined with charms and beads. When adding buttons use a strong thread that matches the button rather than the ground fabric so that the decorative effect is not spoiled.

Other embellishments may be added to your cross stitch designs and include using ribbon roses, tiny artificial flowers and even doll's house miniatures. Why not try adding tiny items of cutlery to a kitchen sampler with buttons for the plates on the dresser and flower-pot charms to the fireplace.

✳ *Beehive* ✳

Stitch Count: 43 x 30
Design Size: 7.5 x 6cm (3 x 2¼in)
Fabric Selection: Half-bleached linen 28 threads to 2.5cm (1in)
Tapestry Needle Size: 24

This pretty little design was stitched using two strands of stranded cottons (floss) for the cross stitch over two threads of linen. French knots were added after the cross stitch was complete using one and two strands of stranded cotton (floss). Finally the brass honey bee charm (see Suppliers) was attached with matching thread. The chart is on page 145 of the Motif Library. See Working the Projects page 126.

✛ Stitch Perfect ✛

• Clean a metal charm thoroughly with a paper towel before applying it to your stitching and if concerned, coat the back of the charm with clear nail polish.

• The size and scale of charms and buttons should match the scale of the cross stitch design.

• Attach charms and buttons using a thread which matches the fabric.

• Starting with a loop start, position the charm (or button) and pass the needle through the hole in the charm from the right side thus marking the position. Slip the charm off the eye of the needle and pass the needle in and out of the fabric and through the loop on the right side. Stitch the charm in position, ensuring that the threads on the needle stay taut and do not form an unsightly loop in the hole of the charm.

• If additional stitches are to be added in direct relationship to the charm or button, stitch the charm in position first and then carefully stitch as shown (see the freehand leaf motif by the dove on the Ark project).

Beads and Cross Stitch

Now that you have learnt the basic skills needed to work counted cross stitch, this section of the book will encourage you to try other exciting options whilst staying with the counted thread concept. Substituting beads for stranded cottons (floss) on parts of a charted design as in the violet design opposite is a wonderful way to begin to explore your creative powers. Working with beads in this way is easier than you can imagine. As all the beads are stitched on using only one colour thread you can work across the pattern row by row instead of working blocks of colour as you would for cross stitch.

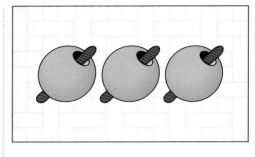

Seed beads are attached using a beading needle or very fine 'sharp' needle and a half cross stitch

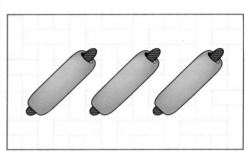

Although bugle beads can be included in a cross stitch pattern, generally they are added to the design after the cross stitch is completed. For example, bugle beads added to the end of the lily stamens on page 23 would add dimension to the project

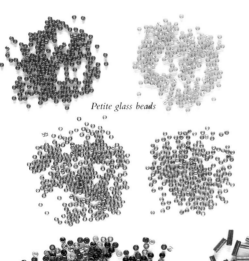

Petite glass beads

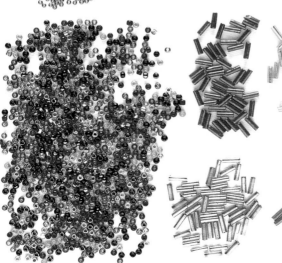

Glass seed beads

Bugle beads

There are dozens of different shapes and sizes of bead available to the stitcher, although, unless you are adding beads at random, you will need to choose beads that are the correct size for the fabric

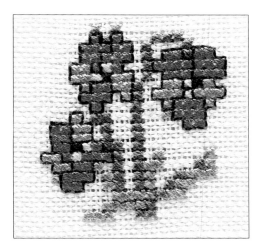

❋ *Violets* ❋

Stitch Count: 18 x 20
Design Size: 3 x 4cm (1¼ x 1½in)
Fabric Selection: Ivory or antique white linen 28 threads to 2.5cm (1in)
Needle size: Tapestry No. 26 and beading needle

This exquisite little design is worked on 28-count ivory linen over two threads, first in cross stitch using DMC stranded cottons (floss), and second replacing the flower colours with seed beads (from Beadesign, see Suppliers). In both cases the stems and leaves are worked in cross stitch over two threads using two strands of stranded cotton (floss). The chart for this design is included in the Motif Library (page 128).

✛ Stitch Perfect ✛

• To substitute beads for stranded cottons (floss) on a chart design, gather together the stranded cottons and match the beads to the threads. Choosing beads in isolation is very difficult.

• Treat bright yellow and orange beads with caution as they can outshine other more subtle colours.

• Apply beads using ordinary sewing thread matched to the fabric colour. To make sure you cannot see the thread through the beads, stitch a few on to the corner of the fabric.

• Remember polyester mixture threads are stronger than pure cotton.

• Choose your fabric carefully. Beads will sit better on evenweave rather than Aida, and on double canvas rather than on single weave.

• Choose beads that are suitable for your fabric count. If the beads are too large the design will distort and the beads will crowd on top of each other. Most seed beads, for example, are perfect for 14 count fabric or canvas (i.e. 14 blocks or 28 threads to 2.5cm (1in)).

• Consider using a frame or a hoop when working with beads. This will keep the fabric taut, and you can pull the thread firmly as you work to keep the beads in position.

Silk Ribbon and Cross Stitch

Adding silk ribbon embroidery to cross stitch can introduce a wonderful new dimension and variety to a piece of stitching, creating a fresh, three-dimensional feel. The Silk Ribbon Sampler illustrated opposite demonstrates the dramatic effect achieved by adding lazy daisy stitches in silk ribbon to the decorative border as well as adding some ribbon French knots to the house. The sampler could be stitched with a cross stitch border if you prefer. The delightful little birdhouse on page 54 also features some ribbon work.

You may wish to try other stitches using silk ribbon such as tent stitch, satin stitch or even bullion stitches and if you are keen to develop the use of silk ribbon in your work it is worth investing in a good ribbon embroidery book (see Bibliography).

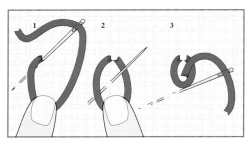

Lazy daisy stitch worked in silk ribbon is very effective when combined with cross stitch. Work the stitch as shown in the diagram, keeping the ribbon untwisted as you form the stitch and don't pull the stitch too tightly

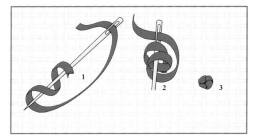

Work the French knot in the same way as described in the Stitch Library (page 116) but use a large gold-plated needle and do not pull the ribbon stitch too tight. You may need to experiment on a spare piece of fabric to perfect your technique

✤ Stitch Perfect ✤

• The use of an embroidery hoop is recommended for silk ribbon embroidery.

• Use a large chenille needle (size 20) for ribbon embroidery, and size 24 tapestry needle when using stranded cotton (floss).

• Work over two threads of the fabric or as stated on the chart.

• Use pure silk ribbon, readily available in 2mm, 3mm or 4mm widths.

• Work with 30cm (12in) lengths of ribbon, cutting the ends at an angle to prevent fraying and make needle threading easier.

• To begin, make a knot at one end of the ribbon and come up through the fabric from the back. Remove any twists in the ribbon before stitching.

• Work with a loose tension to give the required effect – the eye of the size 20 needle should pass under the ribbon with ease.

• When finishing off silk ribbon embroidery, take the ribbon through to the back of the fabric, and using sewing thread, back stitch the end of the ribbon to the nearest stitch of ribbon and then cut off close to the fabric.

• When framing ribbon embroidery, ensure that it does not get squashed by the underside of the glass. Insert very narrow strips of board (spacers) into the edges of the frame, between the glass and the mounted embroidery to hold them apart, before you assemble the frame.

❋ *Silk Ribbon Sampler* ❋

Stitch Count: 100 x 92

Design Size: 18.5 x 17cm ($7^{1}/_{4}$ x $6^{3}/_{4}$in)

Fabric Selection: Zweigart Cashel antique white linen 28 threads to 2.5cm (1in)

Tapestry Needle Size: 24

The sampler is stitched over two threads of linen using two strands of stranded cotton for the cross stitch and one for back stitch, and 2mm silk ribbon from YLI. You can change the initials by using the alphabet in the sampler. The design is charted on page 160/161 of the Motif Library.
See Working the Projects page 126.

Blackwork Embroidery

When designing a sampler, I often like to include sections of blackwork as a contrast to the areas of cross stitch included in a pattern. The name blackwork tends to mislead but the lovely lacy effect achieved can enhance a pure cross stitch pattern.

Blackwork is an embroidery technique consisting of geometric patterns built up using double running (Holbein) stitch (see diagram) and was traditionally worked in black thread against a contrasting (usually white) background with gold metallic highlights added for extra impact. During Elizabethan times blackwork embroidery was used to decorate clothing to imitate the appearance of lace. The name is rather misleading as this type of counted embroidery can be stitched in any colour you choose. Many different effects can be achieved by varying the thickness of the thread, and careful selection of patterns with dark, medium and light tones. You will see from the page of blackwork designs overleaf that you can select different patterns to create the dark and light effects.

Modern blackwork makes good use of different colours and as you can see from the photographs can create amazing effects. The prancing deer is worked in traditional style using black and gold but the holly and berry motif are worked using red and green stranded cotton (floss). As you can see from the illustration, any cross stitch chart can be adapted to suit black-work treatment. I have taken the outline of the black cat on page 76 and worked a blackwork pattern with great success.

✛ Stitch Perfect ✛

• Blackwork is traditionally worked using double running stitch or Holbein stitch, rather than back stitch.

• Holbein stitch will give a smoother effect and the back of your work will look almost as good as the front, so it is particularly useful for table linen.

• Before starting to stitch you will need to plan the direction you are working so that you can return to fill the gaps without ending up a blind alley!

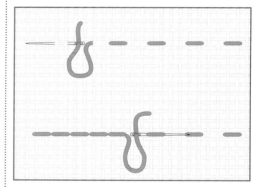

To work double running or Holbein stitch, begin by working a running stitch under and over two threads of evenweave or one block of Aida. Then stitch the return journey, filling in the gaps

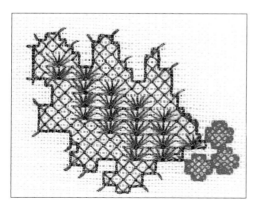

❊ *Holly and Berries* ❊

Stitch Count: 32 x 25
Design Size: 6.5 x 5cm (2¹/₂ x 2in)
Fabric Selection: Antique white linen 28 threads to 2.5cm (1in)
Tapestry Needle Size: 24

The outline of this design was worked in two strands of green stranded cotton (floss) over two threads of linen with the repeating patterns worked in green and red stranded cotton (floss). The chart for this design is included in the Motif Library (page 136) although there are examples of blackwork patterns overleaf on page 62. See Working the Projects page 126.

❋ *Prancing Deer* ❋

Stitch Count: 37 x 37
Design Size: 7.5 x 7.5cm (3 x 3in)
Fabric Selection: Antique white
linen 28 threads to 2.5cm (1in)
Tapestry Needle Size: 26

This blackwork design shows how the outline shape of a motif is worked and then filled with traditional blackwork stitches. The outline was worked in two strands of black stranded cotton (floss) over two threads of the linen with the repeating patterns worked in gold metallic thread and a single strand of black stranded cotton (floss). The chart for this design is in the Motif Library (page 136) although there are further examples of blackwork patterns overleaf on page 62. See Working the Projects page 126.

❋ *Black Cat* ❋

Stitch Count: 66 x 41
Design Size: 12 x 7.5cm (4³/₄ x 3in)
Fabric Selection: Ivory linen 28 threads to 2.5cm (1in)
Tapestry Needle Size: 24

This design uses the chart for the Cat on a Wall, shown on page 76 and charted in the Motif Library on page 138. The outline of the design was worked in two strands of black stranded cotton (floss) over two threads of linen with the repeating pattern worked in one strand of black. See Working the Projects page 126.

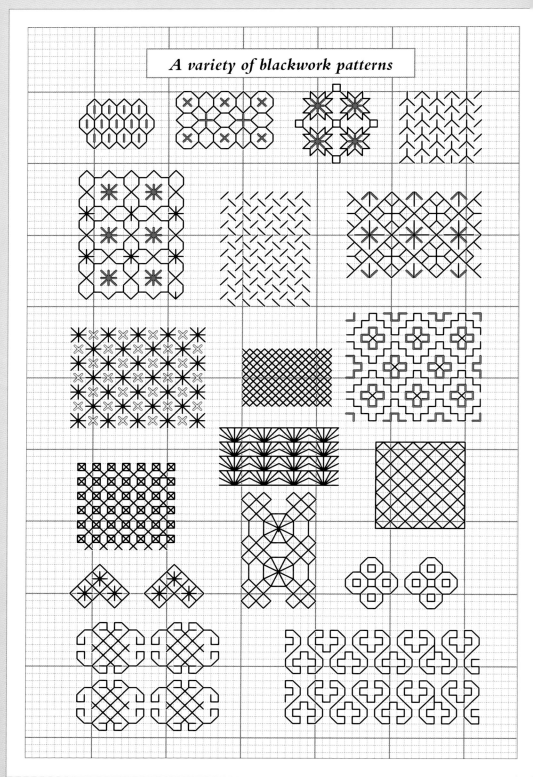

A variety of blackwork patterns

Assisi Embroidery

This style of cross stitch, named after the town in Italy, can be described as pure cross stitch although in reverse. The design is transferred to the fabric by working a back stitch outline first, then the background of the design is stitched leaving the motif shown as blank fabric.

The example in the colour picture below illustrates the versatility of a cross stitch chart because the outline used for the yellow rose on Lurex fabric has been used as the framework for the Assisi rose embroidery using a delicate Caron Waterlilies thread (code 098). You could choose almost any design from the Motif Library and work it in the same way.

✢ Stitch Perfect ✢

• Work the outline in back stitch or Holbein stitch (see page 60), carefully counting from the chart.

• Experiment with the number of strands needed to create the effect required.

• Work the cross stitch in two journeys to keep a neat tension throughout and perfect vertical lines on the reverse. If using a brighter coloured Caron thread with more distinctive colour changes it would be best to work the cross stitches individually.

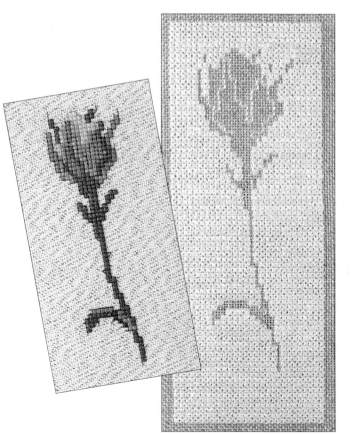

✳ *Assisi Rose* ✳

Stitch Count: 18 x 65
Design Size: 4 x 12cm
($1^1/_2$ x $4^3/_4$in)
Fabric Selection: Unbleached linen
28 threads to 2.5cm (1in)
Tapestry Needle Size: 26

This lovely rose design has been stitched in reverse therefore the stitch count refers to the actual design rather than the completed picture. The flower has been stitched from the chart for the yellow rose on page 146, originally stitched on gold Lurex fabric. Using the back stitch outline only, the design has been left bare whilst the background has been cross stitched in one strand of Caron Waterlilies thread (098). Outlines from other motifs in the Motif Library could be treated in the same way. See Working the Projects page 126.

Counted but Free

It is quite possible to take an original cross stitch chart and to work it in quite a different way to create a textured, almost three-dimensional effect to your stitching. This is achieved by replacing blocks of cross stitch with other counted stitches specially chosen to give the effect of a particular material, for example long stitch can be used to create a thatching effect. These substituted stitches are worked in the same colour stranded cottons (floss) as the original chart, but the end result will be very different. Many cross stitchers are very nervous of any type of free embroidery, but as this technique uses only counted stitches they no longer need to be.

To practise the 'counted but free' approach, simply outline the areas on the original chart that you wish to fill with textured stitches and transfer on to a blank piece of graph paper: you might be able to use the highlighting back stitch lines on the original chart as a start point as I have for the re-worked rose cottage design. Now, using the Stitch Library, choose suitable stitches to recreate the textured effects you are hoping to achieve. Using a different colour for each selected stitch, colour in each block of your outline as a guide, and then get stitching.

Here are some ideas of how to achieve some textures, but have fun experimenting with some of your own.

Bricks	Vertical, diagonal and horizontal satin stitch
Corn Sheaves	Half Rhodes stitch
Flower Heads	Algerian eye
Roses	Bullion bars
Flower Stems	Counted chain stitch

On those occasions that you want to stitch almost at random, in a garden area for instance, select the coloured threads used in the original cross stitch pattern, work a back stitch border around the section, and then add the stitches freely using the colours in a less rigid way. In this way a flower bed could be completely filled with French knots randomly stitched but following the colour guidance of the original design.

✥ Stitch Perfect ✥

• You can use Aida for limited effect when trying the 'counted but free' technique, but to explore the idea fully work on evenweave fabric.

• As the back stitch outline on the fabric will be covered by your 'free' stitches, the shade of thread used for this is unimportant.

• Add further back stitch for definition after some of the free embroidered sections are completed.

• If you are intending to work long stitches or a large amount of satin stitch, a frame or hoop may be useful.

• Try using different thickness of threads when stitching, or silk ribbon or fine wool for an interesting textural effect.

• Choose alternative stitches to match the type of effect you want.

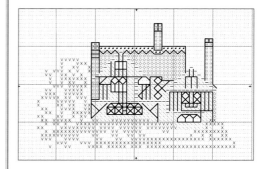

Transfer the back stitch lines from this original cross stitch chart on to graph paper and use these to plan which additional stitches to work within these lines.

✳ *Rose Gable Cottage* ✳

Stitch Count: 51 x 33
Design Size: 9 x 6cm ($3^1/2$ x $2^1/2$in)
Fabric Selection: Ivory linen 28 threads to 2.5cm (1in)
Tapestry Needle Size: 24

Both the cross stitch and 'counted but free' version of this design have been worked in two strands of stranded cotton over two threads of linen. The textured version of the cottage has been worked using the original cross stitch chart as a guide. I outlined the building carefully counting from the chart, but added straw-coloured long stitch for the thatched roof, cream long stitch for the front gables and double cross stitch for the chimneys. After the remainder of the design was completed I added random French knots in greens and pinks on top of the stitching to indicate roses. The original cross stitch design can be found in the Motif Library on page 159.

Pulled Thread and Drawn Thread Work

These two techniques work extremely well with cross stitch, particularly for band samplers, as you can see in the four seasonal samplers shown in the Stitch Library. These beautiful pieces demonstrate the exciting variety of counted stitches and how techniques can be combined. This section is intended to be used in conjunction with the Stitch Library, particularly queen stitch, Algerian eye and hem stitch variations.

There is sometimes confusion between pulled thread work and drawn thread work and a clear explanation of the difference between the two techniques is needed before the stitching can be tackled successfully.

Pulled Thread Work

This refers to a type of embroidery where patterns of holes are created in fabric, usually linen, by *pulling* threads together with various stitches. The holes produced by the pulled-work stitches form patterns that are, perhaps confusingly, referred to as fillings. *No threads are cut or removed in pulled thread work.* Pulled stitches, such as four-sided stitch, Algerian eye, hem stitch and Queen stitch, can be worked alone or with cross stitch to form borders, to create abstract or geometric motifs or as patterns for filling spaces in a design, for example in the four seasonal samplers. A detail from the Summer Sampler shown below illustrates the use of pulled stitches. (See also the following section on Hem Stitching.)

Linen is used for this type of embroidery because the fibres are very strong and even stronger when wet. Linen has a tendency to crease easily, so excess folding and crumpling of the fabric should be avoided but this makes it ideal for pulled-work projects because, when the threads are pulled together, they bend or crease and stay in place, producing the lacy effects of pulled work. Linen is so hardwearing, it is the best choice for projects that require many hours of work, or items that will be used and laundered often.

A detail from the Summer Sampler (page 98) showing some pulled stitches – Queen stitch and Algerian eye

✛ Stitch Perfect ✛
Pulled Thread Work

• Use linen for pulled thread work, particularly for tableware, samplers and pillow covers.

• Pull the stitches so that the threads of the fabric are drawn together to form holes.

• With some stitches in pulled work, e.g. Algerian eye, the central hole is formed by pulling the thread firmly. This takes a little practice in order to produce even holes and tension, and cross stitchers often find this odd at first as they do not distort the fabric normally.

• Examples of pulled stitches are described in the Stitch Library (see page 83 for index) and include Algerian eye, several other eyelet variations, four-sided stitch, queen stitch, hem stitch and variations of hem stitch.

Drawn Thread Work

Drawn thread work may superficially look like pulled work but their methods are quite different because in drawn thread work, *threads are cut and drawn out* from the ground fabric. The technique is often used after hem stitch or four-sided stitch have been worked. (See also the following section on Hem Stitching.) With reference to figs 1–3, you will see that the drawn fabric threads can be treated in one of two ways: they can be cut off after satin stitching or woven into the edge of the fabric to form a selvedge.

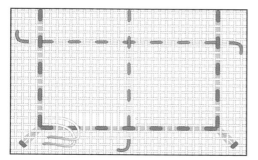

Fig 1 *This shows the fabric with two horizontal threads cut, beginning to be unwoven*

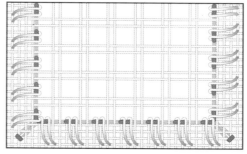

Fig 2 *This shows the cut threads withdrawn to the edge of the fabric*

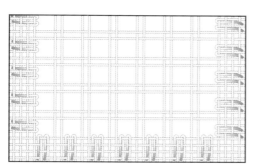

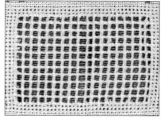

Fig 3 (left) *This shows the cut threads removed and the loose ends woven into the fabric edges*

A detail from the Spring Sampler (page 90) showing some drawn thread work

---

✛ Stitch Perfect ✛
Drawn Thread Work

• If a square of hem stitch or four-sided stitch is worked as in the detail from the Spring Sampler above, alternate pairs of vertical and horizontal linen threads can be cut and pulled back to the hem stitching leaving a two-thread margin.

• Drawn threads are taken to the back of the stitching and tacked out of the way.

• A row of satin stitch is then worked inside the hem stitch square anchoring the threads which are then trimmed away.

• The remaining groups of threads can be decorated with simple wrapping as illustrated or with dove's eye stitch if preferred.

• When bands of hem stitching are worked as shown in this sampler detail, only the horizontal threads are snipped.

• The drawn threads are taken back to the edge of the section and woven in to the body of the fabric leaving vertical threads to be embellished as shown.

Hem Stitching

This section is intended to be used in conjunction with the Stitch Library, particularly pages 111–114. Included within the Stitch Library you will see four samplers, Spring, Summer, Autumn and Winter (pages 90, 98, 108 and 124 respectively), all of which are stitched on linen and include not just cross stitch and a variety of other exciting counted stitches but also the chance to try decorative hem stitching. Hem stitching and other decorative edgings are sometimes referred to as 'finishing'. The hem stitch is a wonderfully versatile stitch allowing you to hem a raw edge, form a folded hem or remove horizontal threads from the fabric leaving the vertical threads to

be decorated. Hem stitching can therefore be purely decorative or functional and works well with pulled work and drawn thread work (see page 66).

You can see from the stitched examples that the art of decorative hem stitching is not difficult but must be worked in stages. The bookmarks on page 51 illustrate the effect of cutting the threads after hem stitching has been worked to form a safe edge. The samples stitched and illustrated here show the folded hem method allowing you to form a neat hem on the wrong side of the fabric showing a delicate pattern of pulled holes on the right side.

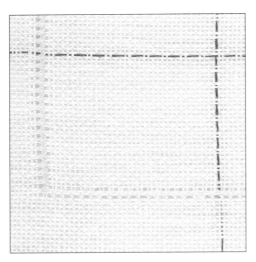

Two rows of hem stitch worked without the withdrawal of any threads but with tacking stitches in place

Hem stitch worked, with alternate threads cut, withdrawn to the hem stitch and tacked out of the way, leaving threads remaining for decoration

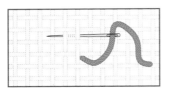
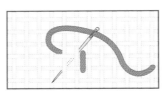
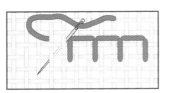

These four diagrams show the stages of working hem stitch, in this case over two threads in each direction. Work a straight stitch over two threads, turning the needle horizontally to create a stitch at right angles. Turn the needle diagonally and repeat the straight and horizontal stitches along the row, counting carefully. After hem stitching, thread withdrawal may take place

✛ Stitch Perfect ✛

- To form a perfect fold when stitching a hem try scoring the fabric. Place the fabric on a clean, flat surface (not French polished) and place the needle in a line of threads which will form the fold. Carefully pull the fabric not the needle which will create a score mark on the fabric making turning the material simple.

- Count the site very carefully and if nervous work a line of tacking threads over and under two threads of the linen prior to thread withdrawal.

- The next step is to cut the thread. Count to the centre of area to be hemmed and snip one horizontal thread once. Then carefully unravel the cut thread from the middle to the edge.

- Weave the linen thread into the side of the fabric as shown below to form a selvedge.

- Using two strands of stranded cotton (floss), work the hem stitch as indicated on a chart taking care to count two threads carefully.

- Start and finish at the end of each section. Do not begin a new thread in the middle of a row.

Stitching a Folded Hem

The most common method is to withdraw a thread across and down the fabric which will, when stitched, form the decorative pattern on the front of the folded hem (see picture right). The withdrawn thread is woven into the fabric at the edge of the hemmed area to form a selvedge. Once the fabric is prepared the raw edge can be folded and the hem stitch worked from the wrong side. When working hem stitch as part of a sampler and for decorative purposes, I prefer to work two rows of hem stitches and then withdraw the threads. Either way is acceptable and depends on the project.

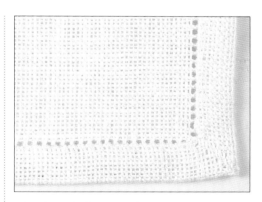

This shows the front view of a hem-stitched corner

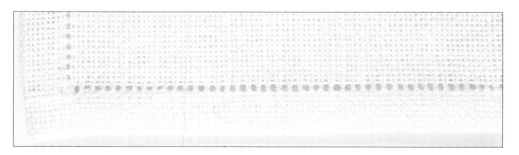

This shows the back or wrong side of a hem-stitched corner, showing the fold

Hardanger Embroidery

Hardanger embroidery or cut work is easy to do and is extremely effective when combined with cross stitch but it seems to strike terror in the hearts of all cross stitchers, possibly because they have snipped a fabric thread in error whilst unpicking!

Hardanger, a town in Norway, gave its name to this type of counted embroidery, where cut work was a feature of the local dress. This section of the book is intended to give you a taste of Hardanger embroidery and if you find that you want to experiment further there is an excellent guide listed in the Bibliography.

This section is intended to be used in conjunction with the Stitch Library, particularly pages 120 to 123.

At its simplest, Hardanger work basically consists of three stages which are described over the next few pages:

1 Stitching Kloster blocks.
2 Cutting threads.
3 Decorating the remaining threads and spaces.

The secret of successful cut work embroidery is working Kloster blocks (the framework needed for the decorative filling stitches) and to count the Kloster blocks correctly. If they are in the right place the threads may be cut out and the stitching will not fall to pieces!

Hardanger embroidery may be worked on evenweave fabric of any thread count or on Hardanger fabric which is supplied with 22 blocks to 2.5cm (1in). If working on Hardanger fabric, treat each block as one thread.

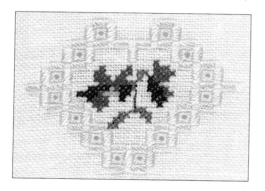

✽ *Hardanger Violet Coaster* ✽
Stitch Count: 38 x 30
Design Size: 7 x 5cm (2³/₄ x 2in) excluding buttonhole stitched edge
Fabric Selection: Ivory linen 28 threads to 2.5cm (1in)
Tapestry Needle Size: 24 and 22

The heart shape in this coaster has been created with Kloster blocks worked in cotton perlé, with the eyelet stitches worked in two strands of stranded cotton (floss), creating decorative holes without any cutting of threads (see Pulled Thread Work on page 66). The violet cross stitch motif has been stitched using two strands of stranded cotton (floss) from a chart on page 153 of the Motif Library. This project could be completed with the buttonhole edging and cut out as illustrated on page 73.

(see Pulled Thread Work on page 66); page 153 of the Motif Library; illustrated on page 73.

✛ Stitch Perfect ✛
Kloster Blocks

• To form Kloster blocks, work the stitches side by side so that they look the same on the wrong side of the fabric.

• The vertical and horizontal blocks must meet at the corners, sharing the corner hole.

• Check that you have counted correctly as you stitch and check that each block is in the correct position.

• Check that vertical Kloster blocks are opposite one another and horizontal blocks are opposite horizontal ones.

• Work all the Kloster blocks in a pattern, checking that the blocks meet where they should.

• Never start cutting until the Kloster blocks are completed and match everywhere.

• Do not travel between blocks at the back unless under existing Kloster blocks.

Stitching Kloster Blocks

Kloster blocks form the framework for the cut areas in Hardanger embroidery. They are worked in patterns, formed with 5 vertical or 5 horizontal straight stitches, each of them over 4 threads on evenweave or 4 blocks if working on Hardanger fabric. The stitches are worked side by side, following the grain of the fabric (see fig 1). Do not let thread cross over open space on the back of the fabric (see fig 2).

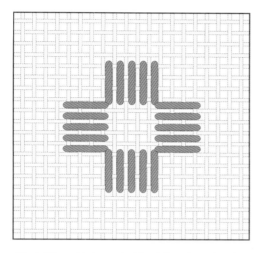

Fig 1 Kloster blocks worked but left without threads cut and removed (shows the right side)

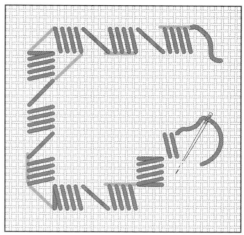

Fig 2 Kloster blocks from the wrong side - the red route is to be avoided

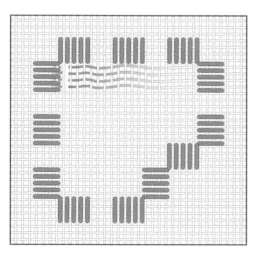

Fig 3 Kloster blocks stitched, with some threads cut awaiting withdrawal

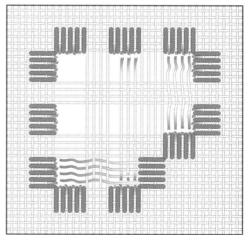

Fig 4 Kloster blocks stitched with some threads cut and some withdrawn

Cutting Threads

When the Kloster blocks have been stitched, the threads between them are cut and drawn out. The secret to successful cutting is to work *all* the Kloster blocks, checking that you have counted correctly and that all the blocks are exactly opposite each other. Looking at the photographs of the Hardanger heart opposite you can see that the Kloster blocks are formed in vertical and horizontal lines. The threads should be cut, in pairs, with very sharp, pointed scissors at the end of the Kloster blocks, as shown in fig 3 (page 71), not at the side. Remember to cut where the needle has pierced the fabric. Withdraw the cut threads carefully (see fig 4) and when all the cut threads are removed the work should look like fig 5 (and the second stage of the Hardanger Heart coaster opposite).

If you do make a mistake and cut a thread unintentionally it is easy to correct this. Just remove the fabric thread you've cut by mistake, then take a strand of stranded cotton (floss) the same colour as your fabric and darn it in and out so that it replaces the accidentally cut thread leaving a long thread hanging on the wrong side. Needleweave or wrap this section next to anchor the threads, then the loose thread can be trimmed.

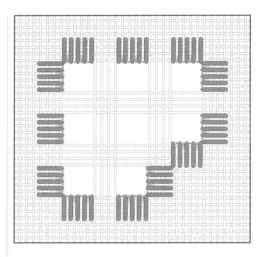

Fig 5 Kloster blocks stitched and with all the correct threads cut and withdrawn ready for decorating. After cutting, do not worry if you can see some small whiskers at the cut sites. Leave these until the piece is finished. Many will withdraw as the work is handled, but if necessary they can be carefully trimmed when the piece is complete

---

✤ Stitch Perfect ✤
Cutting Threads

- Work slowly, in a good light and with small, pointed, sharp scissors.

- The cutting side is where the long straight stitches enter the fabric. *Never* cut alongside the long edges of the stitches.

- Cut the threads at the end of each Kloster block, working from a corner outwards. You will be cutting four threads, but cut them in twos.

- Pass the point of the scissors into the corner-shared hole and lift the threads.

- Check that you can see both points of the scissors and that you are only cutting two threads, then lean slightly towards the Kloster block and cut.

- It is easier to cut all the relevant threads in one direction first then turn the fabric to cut in another direction.

- Pull out the loose threads using tweezers if necessary. The stitching should look like the second photograph (opposite) with groups of four threads vertically and horizontally left to decorate.

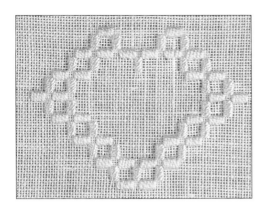

This first stage shows the Kloster blocks completed

This shows the back of the stitching to show that the Kloster blocks should look similar back and front

This second stage shows the fabric threads cut and withdrawn, ready to be decorated

✳ Hardanger Heart Coaster ✳

Stitch Count: 42 x 38
Design Size: 7.5 x 7cm (3 x 2³/₄in)
Fabric Selection: Ivory linen 28 threads to 2.5cm (1in)
Tapestry Needle Size: 22

This exquisite Hardanger Heart Coaster has been stitched using one strand of perlé cotton No.5 in ecru for the Kloster blocks and the buttonhole edging. After the Kloster blocks were completed, the fabric threads were cut and withdrawn. The needleweaving and dove's eyes were then worked using one strand of ecru perlé cotton No.8. The chart is on page 153 of the Motif Library.

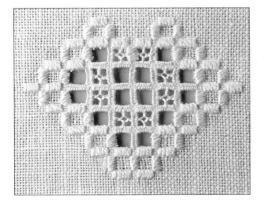

The third stage showing base threads and void areas completed with needleweaving and dove's eyes

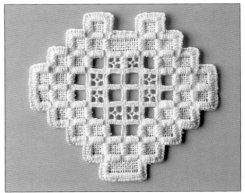

The Hardanger Heart Coaster with a buttonhole edging completed and excess fabric cut away

Decorating Threads and Voids

When Kloster blocks are completed and the threads are cut and removed, you are left with groups of threads and spaces, void areas, to strengthen and decorate (see fig 5 page 72). There are many ways to do this but there is only room to give you a taste of Hardanger embroidery here and in the Stitch Library so only the basic principles will be covered.

Needleweaving (see Stitch Library page 122 for full instructions) is one of the most commonly used methods of embellishing threads left after cutting, especially over larger areas, and creates covered bars (see fig 6) which can be worked alone or combined with filling stitches such as dove's eye and picots. When needleweaving use a slightly finer thread than for stitching Kloster blocks.

Wrapped bars (see Stitch Library page 120 for full instructions) are also used to embellish threads left after cutting (see fig 7). They may be worked alone or as part of other decorative stitches such as spider's webs.

Filling stitches (see Stitch Library pages 121 and 123 for full instructions) are used to decorate the voids left by cutting threads. Some of the basic ones you might like to try include dove's eye stitch, spider's web stitch and picots.

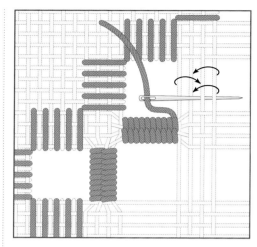

Fig 6 Needleweaving – full instructions page 122

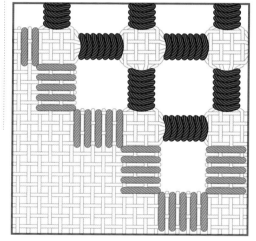

Fig 7 Wrapped bars – full instructions page 120

✣ Stitch Perfect ✣
Needleweaving

- When needleweaving use a slightly finer thread than for stitching the Kloster blocks.

- To weave a bar, bring the needle up in a void area and work over and under pairs of threads.

- After completing one bar, weave the next one at right angles to it, working around the design, taking care not to run threads across the back of the cut areas.

- Needleweaving shouldn't alter the shape of the bar, which should stay flat and straight.

✳ *Hardanger Flower Chatelaine,* ✳ *Scissors Keeper and Needlecase*

Stitch Count: see small designs in Motif Library page 162
Fabric Selection: Ivory linen band 6cm (2¹/₂in) wide and ivory linen 28 threads to 2.5cm (1in)
Tapestry Needle Size: 24 and 22

These items were worked over two linen threads, using stranded cotton (floss) (two strands), perlé cotton (one strand) and Caron Watercolours (093 or 171) thread (one strand). The scissors keeper and needlecase are charted on page 162. The chatelaine uses motifs from pages 162 and 136. You could work them as shown here or rearrange the elements in a design of your own.

Adapting Chart Designs

There can be no better introduction to cross stitch than working one of the many small kits available. However, there is no reason why the more experienced embroiderer should not enjoy these too. They are still the cheapest way to collect the essentials to complete a picture, and they can provide the perfect opportunity to develop simple designing techniques using the chart from the kit as a starting point. It is possible, with just a little imagination, to create many new designs from the original provided, and the photograph opposite shows what a difference can be made by adapting just a few basic elements.

✕✕✕✕✕

✳ *Cat on a Wall* ✳

Stitch Count: 99 x 56
Design Size: 18 x 11cm (7 x 4¹/₄in)
Fabric Selection:
Above: 16-count Aida
Below: Ivory linen 28 threads to 2.5cm (1in)
Tapestry Needle Size: 24

The small cross stitch kit can offer the perfect opportunity for the stitcher to begin to develop their design skills as they adapt the chart to their own preferences. The picture opposite shows one of my bestselling cross stitch kits. Above, the stitching has been completed on 16-count Aida exactly matching the picture on the kit front. Below, the design has been stitched again, this time on ivory linen, but with some distinctive changes. The black and white cat remains the same, but the wall has changed from brick to old stone and is now decorated with random French knot roses. I photocopied the original cross stitch chart, slightly enlarged it and wrote notes to myself directly onto it to remind me of what I intended to do. I exchanged the red brick for Cotswold stone shades and added extra greenery to square off the end of the design. The French knots were added at random after the cross stitch was complete. The chart for my new version can be found in the Motif Library on page 138.

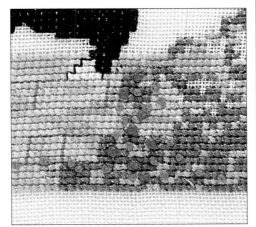

✦ First Steps to Design ✦

People buy ready-made cross stitch kits partly for convenience and partly to avoid making design decisions. This section will start you thinking of ways to change and personalise kits — the beginning of designing for yourself.

- Consider adding names and dates to the finished piece to make it unique.

- To add wording, draw the letters on to a clean sheet of graph paper, mark the centre, then stitch in position.

- Look at the picture of the kit design and try a simple change of colour. You may prefer a blue and gold border rather than pink and gold, for example.

- Always make a copy of the original chart, and write yourself notes on to this. Keep the notes simple, e.g. 'French knots here' — the colours and detail can come as you stitch.

- Keep records of what colour was used for each change so that you can ensure that both sides of the design match if this is crucial.

- Avoid adding too many different colours to a pattern: instead use different shades of the same colour.

- When you have tried these simple tips to experiment with altering purchased kits, consider: is it time to try designing for yourself?

Designing a Sampler

There are whole books devoted to embroidery design so this section can only give you some basic tips on how to start designing your own work. If you wish to begin with a simple project, such as the sampler shown here, then it might be useful to remember that a sampler usually contains the following elements:

- A border round the design.
- A selection of motifs or patterns within the border, which may be single or mirror image and may reflect a specific theme.
- An alphabet and perhaps a set of numbers.
- Some initials or a name and date.

There are many borders in the Motif Library that you could use for your own sampler or piece of work. Of course you could design your own border, either a simple one as I did here and for the Traditional Cross Stitch Sampler on page 82, or a more complicated border, perhaps to reflect the theme you have chosen for your sampler (e.g., the Acorn and Flower Sampler on page 33).

You can make borders turn corners by placing a small mirror at a 45 degree angle to a border and moving it along until a satisfactory corner is reflected in the mirror. This corner can then be copied onto graph paper. Alternatively you could leave the corners open, stopping the border just short.

Your choice of motifs or patterns to use in a sampler needs to take into account various things - who the embroidery is for, whether the motifs should reflect a particular theme, and your own personal preferences as to style and colour. There are hundreds and hundreds of charted motifs available commercially which you can use in your designs and adapt in various ways (see Adapting Chart designs page 77). If you wish to chart your own drawing of an image simply copy it onto tracing graph paper and then square off the design and colour it in. If the image is the wrong size to begin with you could enlarge or reduce it on a photocopier before you start to square it off.

As with motifs and patterns, there are many books available with all sorts of charted alphabets and number styles for you to use in your embroidery. If composing a line of text or verse, use graph paper to initially plan out the letters to ensure the spacing looks pleasing. Initials used could be your own or the recipients.

Basic Design Decisions

When designing for the first time the idea may seem daunting but try dealing with it in small, bite-sized pieces. You will need to make fairly basic decisions before you start work.

- What size do you want your piece of work to be? A sampler can be any size or shape, generally determined by how much time you have to stitch and if you have a special deadline.
- Are you planning to work the design entirely in cross stitch or use additional stitches as well?
- What is the end use of your piece of stitching? A sampler does not have to be made into a picture – a small design might look well in a card or even as a pincushion.
- Are you designing a traditional piece or one with a more modern feel? This will affect what motifs you choose and how you combine them, particularly for a traditional sampler, where it is important to select motifs which are of the right style and weight. An extreme example would be adding a Ferrari car to a traditional border and stylised trees and flowers!
- When selecting a house motif, relate the size and style of the house to any figures included and adjust the choices of flowers and trees to suit the overall plan.
- A balance needs to be achieved between the motifs you select and the size of the overall design. A large heavy alphabet may be better on its own rather than part of a mixed sampler.
- When designing a large sampler project consider selecting a deep, strong border rather than a narrow, rather mean style. Use the simple narrow border designs around smaller projects.
- Is the design intended to be read like a verse or a prayer? If so the style of the letters must be kept simple or they may be difficult to read. (Look through the Motif Library for ideas.)
- Check dates and the spelling of names when including them in your stitching. We have all made mistakes!
- If you are selecting a motif for a card or trinket pot, make sure that the design will fit the aperture.

Selecting Fabric

The next stage in the process could be to select the fabric type you wish to work on, considering the following:

✳ *Simple Sampler* ✳
Stitch Count: 61 x 83
Design Size: 11.5 x 15cm
(4$^{1}/_{2}$ x 6in)
Fabric Selection: Pure linen
28 threads to 2.5cm (1in)
Tapestry Needle Size: 24

This tiny traditional sampler was worked in two strands of stranded cotton (floss) over two threads of the linen fabric. The initials added are taken from the alphabet on the sampler so you can replace these with initials of your choice. (See page 80 for ways of personalising your work.) The chart is on page 149 of the Motif Library. See Working the Projects page 126.

- Whether the design is very traditional and would suit an evenweave rather than an Aida fabric.
- Your eyesight and the amount of time you have to complete the stitching.
- The overall size of the chart you have created and the need for a high stitch count ie 18-count Aida.
- Whether your chart includes a large number of three-quarter cross stitches (which are easier to stitch on evenweave than on Aida).

Design Content
Now you are ready to decide on the actual content of your design so you will need to consider the following:
- Before you start planning a sampler you need to consider doing a little research. Is the design for a family member or special friend and is it a secret?
- Consider referring to older or more distant relatives for family details. Draw out the family tree to include the receiver.
- If planning a local design to include maps or plans, use libraries to collect information about the local area.
- Make lists of the receiver's hobbies and favourite pastimes.
- Don't be afraid to experiment with using different motifs. Trial and error will achieve the most successful results. You could have a master chart on which you can temporarily stick motifs to judge the overall effect.

Having read all the above don't be disheartened by the work involved because the pleasure and pride you will feel when your own design is stitched and framed will be overwhelming! Whether the sampler is for yourself, a family member or a friend, the feeling of achievement will outweigh the anguish of designing and stitching it!

Personalising Your Work

Many cross stitch charts and purchased kits, particularly samplers, include somewhere to add the name of the stitcher and possibly the date completed or the date of the special occasion for which it was stitched. This is a very important part of our responsibility when a piece of work is completed, to leave some information about the piece of work. Designs worked on linen will certainly be here when we are gone and it would be so helpful, not to mention interesting, to a descendant if some information was available.

✛ Stitch Perfect ✛

- If you do not wish to include your full name on a project, you could add your initials and the date, out of sight but inside the frame.

- You may wish to include a simple trade mark. I know one designer who adds a tiny flower head amongst the design!

- When framing a completed piece, why not write a paragraph about the design, its date and how it came to be. Add your own details and pop it inside the back of the frame.

- Why not draw a simple label ready to stick on the back of completed framed pieces along these lines:

  Designed and stitched by …
  Completed and presented on…
  On the occasion of …

You could also add notes on why you wanted to design the project and how you collected the information.

- Take a photograph of work you are giving away so that you can keep a record.

Designing Monograms

This technique, an excellent way of constructing your own trade mark, is very simple to do and can be stitched quickly, ideal for the emergency present or card. The monograms stitched opposite are worked from the alphabets in the Motif Library pages 134–135 and any letters in any colour and thread type may be combined to great effect. (These were inspired by monograms designed by Brenda Keyes of the Sampler Company, a UK designer and author.)

✛ Stitch Perfect ✛

- You can use letters from different alphabets but check that they are of similar style and size.

- Copy the letters you require on to two pieces of squared paper.

- Tape one letter to the window and add the second sheet so that you can see both letters at the same time. Rearrange the letters until you are happy with them.

- Copy the letter on the bottom sheet on to the top sheet using a different colour pen.

- As you can see from the stitched examples on page 81, the letters look more effective if some of the curves in the letters intertwine.

❊ *Monograms* ❊

Stitch Count: depends on letters
selected
Fabric Selection: Linen 28 threads
to 2.5cm (1in)
Tapestry Needle Size: 24

These are some simple monogram designs stitched on linen from the two alphabets included in the Motif Library (see pages 134-135).

Computer-Aided Design

Since I started using a computer, people (not stitchers) have asked me what I do with the spare time! Having a computer has changed my working life but perhaps not in the way people think. I do not use a scanner to produce my cross stitch patterns (purely because I can always tell when a design is scanned) so I use a computer to take the drudgery out of designing. When designing a lovely complicated border I can spend time perfecting the pattern repeat rather than spending time copying or tracing mirror images. The computer replaces the pen, paper, scissors, Tipp-ex and eraser but does not 'produce' designs by magic.

If you have access to a computer and wish to try designing for yourself there are a number of dedicated cross stitch programmes from which to select. The various stitching and embroidery magazines available are a good place to start looking for information and advertisements.

Before choosing the correct programme ask yourself the following questions:
- What type of computer do I need?
- How much money am I prepared to spend on the programme?
- How much computer memory is necessary for the programme of my choice?
- Are the designs I produce going to be used professionally or for my own enjoyment?
- Am I going to convert designs into charts using a scanner?
- Do I want to create designs including stitches other than cross stitch?
- Will I need to send my designs to other people, magazines or publishers?
- Will the programme allow me to send charts via e-mail?
- Will the programme allow me to print in colour and black and white.
- Can the programme of my choice be upgraded as technology improves?

✳ Traditional Cross Stitch Sampler ✳

Stitch Count: 78 x 98
Design Size: 14.5 x 17.5cm (5³/₄ x 7in)
Fabric Selection: Antique white linen 28 threads to 2.5cm (1in)
Tapestry Needle Size: 24

This is an example of how to combine two different stitches from the cross stitch family. The cross stitch was worked over two threads and the double cross stitch over four threads of the fabric, all worked using two strands of stranded cotton (floss). The chart is on page 142/143 of the Motif Library. See Working the Projects page 126.

Stitch Library

This personal selection of stitches has been developed and selected over a number of years as I have continued to be an avid cross stitcher but one who enjoys adding and or embellishing her work with other counted stitches and even a little cut work and drawn thread embroidery. In most cases the stitches included in the Stitch Library may be stitched on Aida, evenweave or canvas unless otherwise stated, although some pulled stitches are not as effective when worked on Aida fabric. Some of the stitches illustrated show the stitch worked over two or four fabric threads. Remember that when working the stitch, the construction will stay the same but the size and number of fabric threads used may alter. Always refer to the chart for the correct number of fabric threads involved.

Each stitch in the Stitch Library is first shown enlarged, so you can see exactly what the stitch looks like. There are other photographs showing the stitch in a piece of work featured in the book, plus clear diagrams showing exactly how to work the stitch. Some of the captions to the diagrams are numbered to indicate that there are several steps to working the stitch.

To help you find the stitch you want within the Library, the stitches have been grouped in families and an index is also included here.

×××××

Index of Stitches

Cross Stitch

This simple little stitch, the most important and most commonly used stitch in this book, is the key to counted embroidery. A cross stitch, though very simple, can look exquisite or rather untidy and the following guidelines are to ensure that your stitches are just perfect! Even if you have stitched for years see what you think of the following tips.

Cross Stitch on Aida Fabric

Cross stitch on Aida fabric is normally worked over one block. The cross stitches can be worked singly or in two journeys. It doesn't matter which method you use but make sure that all the top stitches face the same direction.

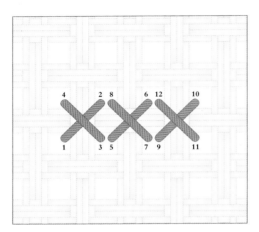

To work a complete cross stitch, follow the numbered sequence, bringing the needle up through the Aida fabric at the bottom left corner of the stitch, cross one block of the fabric and insert the needle at the top right corner. Push the needle through, then bring it up at the bottom right-hand corner, ready to complete the stitch in the top left-hand corner. To work the adjacent stitch, bring the needle up at the bottom right-hand corner of the first stitch.

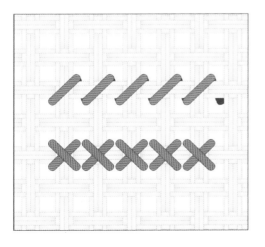

To work cross stitches in two journeys, work the first leg of the cross stitch as above but instead of completing the stitch, work the adjacent half stitch and continue on to the end of the row. Complete all the crosses by working the other diagonals on the return journey.

Cross Stitch on Evenweave Fabric

Stitching on evenweave fabric, such as linen, is no more difficult than stitching on Aida fabric – you only need to be able to count to two! To work a cross stitch on evenweave, follow the instructions given for Aida but work across *two* threads of evenweave fabric instead of one block of Aida, only counting the threads, not the holes.

✕✕✕✕✕

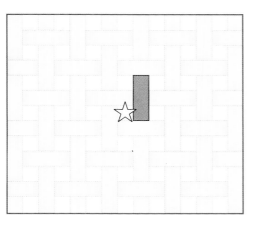

When working on a single weave fabric (an evenweave such as linen), start stitching to the left of a vertical thread. This makes it easier to see when you have made a mistake in counting, because every stitch will start in the same position relevant to adjacent threads of the fabric, making mistakes easy to spot.

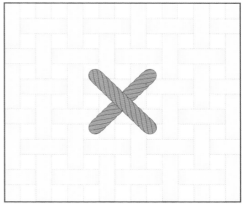

As with Aida you can work complete cross stitches on evenweave one at a time.

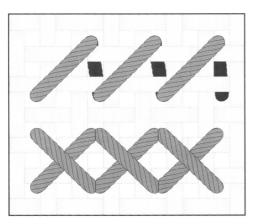

Cross stitches can also be worked on evenweave as rows in two journeys. This is a quicker method and creates a neater appearance on the wrong side, as the photograph (right) shows.

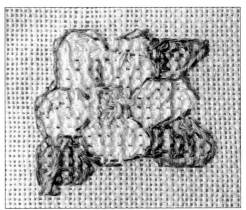

This shows the wrong side of the Christmas rose motif included in the Winter Sampler on page 124. The cross stitch has been worked in two journeys, thus forming neat vertical lines on the reverse.

Three-Quarter Cross Stitch

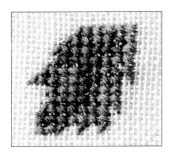

Three-quarter cross stitch is a fractional stitch which helps to produce the illusion of curves when working cross stitch designs. This stitch, a modern addition to the cross stitcher's repertoire, can completely alter the style of your stitching. It is not always popular with stitchers, generally because it is attempted on Aida fabric and it is really intended for evenweave. The stitch can be formed on either material but if you are planning a project that includes many three-quarter cross stitches, do try evenweave, as the formation of the cross stitch leaves a vacant hole for the fractional stitch.

✕✕✕✕✕

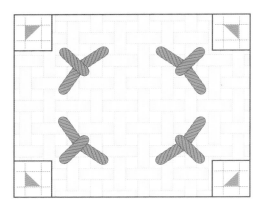

To work a three-quarter cross stitch, work the first half of the cross stitch as usual, sloping the stitch in the direction shown on the chart you are using. Always work the second 'quarter' stitch over the top and down into the central hole to anchor the first half of the stitch. If using Aida, you will need to push the needle through the centre of a block of the fabric.

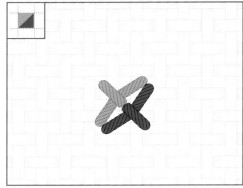

Where two three-quarter stitches lie back-to-back in the space of one full cross stitch, work both of the respective 'quarter' stitches into the central hole.

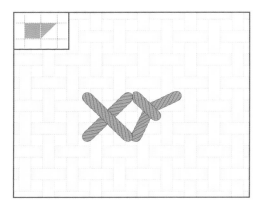

Working a three-quarter cross stitch alongside a full cross stitch.

These pretty pointed leaves could not have been achieved without the use of three-quarter cross stitches. They would have needed to be much larger and much less delicate looking.

Reversible Cross Stitch

There are a number of versions of this stitch but although they are often described as reversible they may not have cross stitch on both sides but create four-sided stitches or a braid-like effect on the back. This stitch is truly reversible, although it has the addition of a vertical line at the end of a row which cannot be avoided. The stitch is quite time consuming as each row is worked four times but it is very useful for book-marks and table linen. The vertical line created at the end of rows can appear as the back stitch outline if you plan your route carefully.

✕✕✕✕✕

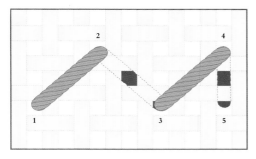

1 *The first journey across two threads on the front of the fabric, working diagonally across the back of the next two threads, missing the stitch on the front.*

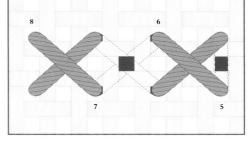

2 *The return journey shows covering the first diagonal threads on the front and back of the work.*

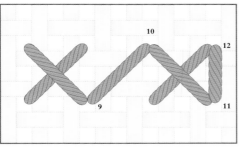

3 *The third journey filling missed stitches back and front.*

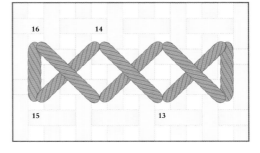

4 *The final journey completing the row.*

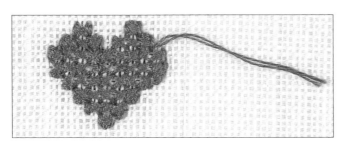

This picture shows the back of the little red heart shown at the top of the page. Reversible cross stitch takes a little time but looks very effective if both sides are to be seen.

Double Cross Stitch
Also known as Smyrna or Leviathan stitch

Double cross stitch may be worked over two or four threads of an evenweave fabric or over two blocks of Aida, to create a series of bold crosses or 'stars'. Tiny double cross stitches may be formed over two threads of evenweave but they are difficult to work on one block of Aida. To keep all double cross stitches uniform make sure that the direction of the stitches within them is the same.

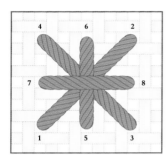

To work a double cross stitch, start to the left of a vertical thread and following the numbered sequence, work a diagonal cross stitch and then add a vertical cross on top.

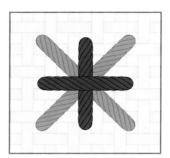

The second vertical cross may be worked in a different colour to add interest if you prefer, in which case work the stitch in two stages – all lower crosses first, followed by the top crosses.

Tiny double cross stitches may be formed over two threads of evenweave in a single colour. Their small size makes them unsuitable for Aida fabric.

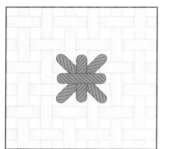

Vertical Double Cross Stitch

Vertical double cross stitch may be worked in two colours in the same way as described for the diagonal version above.

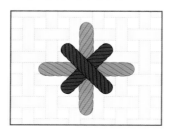

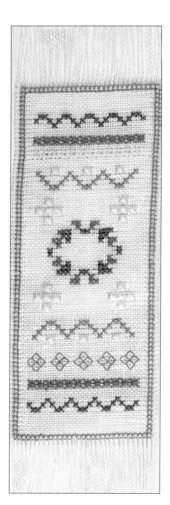

This is one of two bookmarks worked on pure linen (see page 51). This one is stitched in stranded cotton and includes double cross stitch as one of the decorative bands.

Long-Legged Cross Stitch
Also known as long-armed Slav stitch and Portuguese stitch

Long-legged cross stitch seems very uninteresting when first seen but looks wonderful when worked in rows because it forms a plaited braid effect which is ideal for borders, or for the outside edges of pieces to be made up as a pincushion or a scissors keeper. Long-legged cross stitch can also be worked on Aida across two blocks and upwards over one. The stitch may be used to join sections, as shown below.

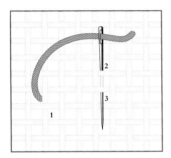

1 *To work long-legged cross stitch on evenweave, begin to the left of a vertical thread. Following the numbered sequence, insert the needle four threads forwards and two threads upwards in a long diagonal 'leg'.*

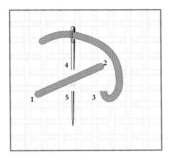

2 *Insert the needle two threads upwards and two threads backwards diagonally to make the short leg.*

This detail illustrates the lovely braid effect produced by long-legged cross stitch, in this case using six strands of stranded cotton (floss) to form the stitches.

3 *To work a row of long-legged cross stitch, follow the numbered sequence shown in the diagram below.*

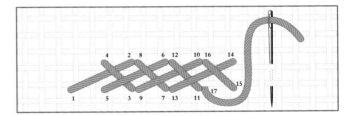

Long-legged Cross Stitch as a Joining Stitch

Long-legged cross stitch is invaluable as it can be used to join two pieces of work as shown in the diagram here. It is easy to do when working on canvas but can also be stitched on Aida or linen effectively.

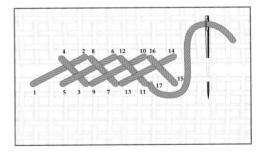

To join two pieces of work using long-legged cross stitch, the sections to be joined need to be folded along a row of threads and then stitched, picking up threads from either side of the gap as illustrated.

✳ The Spring Sampler ✳

Stitch Count: 88 x 159
Design Size: 16.5 x 29cm (6½ x 11½in)
Fabric Selection: Zweigart Cashel linen 28 threads to 2.5cm (1in)
Tapestry Needle Size: 24–22

This is the first of four seasonal samplers included in this section of the book. It is worked as a band sampler and the stitches needed are described on the chart on pages 166-168 and include cross stitch, back stitch and a number of more unusual counted stitches, pulled thread work and Hardanger embroidery. All the stitches in this sampler are included in the Stitch Library but I recommend that you also read Pulled and Drawn Thread Work and Hardanger Embroidery (pages 66 and 70) before starting to stitch.

The chart is over three pages with no over-lapping. You might find it easiest to photocopy the parts and tape them together.

Using stranded cottons (floss) unless other-wise stated, work the cross stitch first, followed by the other counted stitches and then the Hardanger and other pulled or drawn stitches. Refer to the Stitch Library for the stitch diagrams and relevant instructions as you need them.

Work the Bands as follows:

- Use two strands of stranded cotton (floss) for the full and three-quarter cross stitches, double cross stitch, Algerian eye, French knots, palest-rina knots, stem stitch, hem stitch and Queen stitch.
- Use three strands of stranded cotton for the satin stitch.
- Add back stitch outline where required, using one strand of the colour indicated on the chart.
- Where rice stitch is worked in two colours, work the large cross over *four* threads in two strands of stranded cotton (floss) and add the small stitches in *one* strand of gold metallic.
- Add the random French knots in stranded cotton to the blossom trees after completing the cross stitch on the tree.

- Work the cut work section by working two rows of hem stitch around the rectangle as shown on the chart. Referring to the Pulled and Drawn Thread Work page 66, snip alternate pairs of threads vertically and horizontally and carefully un-do the threads back to the edge of the square leaving a two-thread margin. Tack these loose threads out of the way (as illustrated on page 68).
- Using one strand of perlé cotton No. 8 in ecru, and working either across or down the square, needleweave the remaining threads, adding picots and dove's eyes where marked.
- Work the somersault stitch section by working two rows of hem stitch following the chart. Working from the centre of the hem-stitched box, carefully snip each horizontal linen thread *down the centre line* once and using a needle, un-pick the linen threads back to the two outside edges and carefully weave the threads into the fabric thus forming a selvedge. You should be left with vertical threads only.
- Referring to the diagrams on page 113 work two rows of somersault stitch in the same shade as the hem stitch as indicated. Take care to keep the central lines straight and avoid excessive handling to prevent distortion (as seen here).

Work the Hardanger as follows:

- Work the Kloster blocks using one strand of perlé cotton No. 5, counting over four threads of the linen. Keep checking that the blocks are directly opposite each other, referring to the diagrams as necessary.
- When all the Kloster blocks are complete, use very sharp, pointed scissors to cut across the ends of the blocks as shown. Take this section slowly, counting and cutting two threads each time.
- Needleweave the remaining linen threads using one strand of perlé cotton No. 8, adding dove's eyes and picots as indicated.

Rhodes Stitch

Rhodes stitch gives a solid, slightly raised, three-dimensional effect, almost like a series of 'studs' on the fabric. It is particularly successful when worked in thread which has a sheen, to emphasise areas of light and shade. The diagrams illustrate one version but the size of the stitch can be altered to suit your purposes depending how many threads are included. This stitch does not work well on Aida. Check the chart to see how many threads are in each stitch.

✕✕✕✕✕

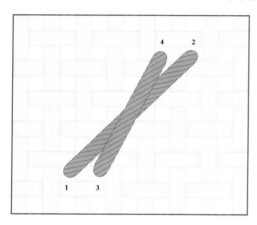

1 *To work a Rhodes stitch begin to the left of a vertical thread, working each stitch over squares of two, four or more threads of evenweave fabric. (Rhodes stitch does not work well on Aida fabric.)*

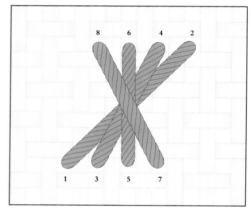

2 *Build the stitch up, working in an anticlockwise direction around the square.*

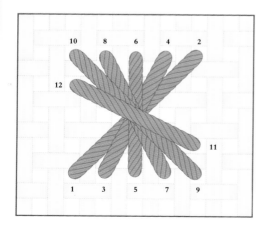

3 *As the numbered sequence is followed, the centre of the stitch becomes raised.*

4 *A completed Rhodes stitch. Maintain the same sequence for every stitch for a uniform effect.*

Half Rhodes Stitch with Bar

This is an adaptation of Rhodes stitch, producing a decorative stitch shaped rather like an old-fashioned sheaf of corn, with a straight bar across the centre to tie the threads together. Buttonhole stitching could be added to the bar.

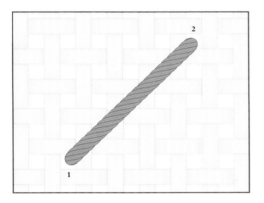

1 *Half Rhodes stitch is worked over squares of two, four, six or eight threads of evenweave fabric, in an anticlockwise direction, slanting as for Rhodes stitch.*

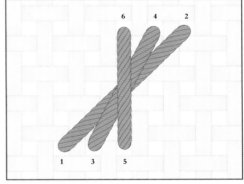

2 *Follow the numbered sequence shown but only working the vertical stages.*

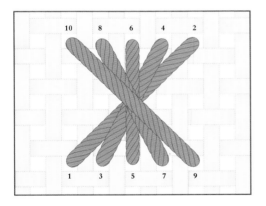

3 *Complete the half Rhodes stitch and maintain the same sequence for every stitch to achieve a uniform effect.*

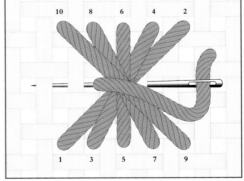

4 *To finish a half Rhodes stitch with a bar, add a single straight stitch across the centre, holding the threads firmly. Add the optional buttonhole stitch (see page 115) across the bar as shown, taking care not to include any of the main stitch as you work. The bar and buttonhole stitching could be worked in a different colour from the half Rhodes stitch to create an interesting alternative.*

Rice Stitch

Rice stitch is a cross stitch with an additional stitch worked over each 'leg' or corner of the cross. It can be worked in two stages: a row of normal cross stitches, followed by the additional stitches as a second row. This makes it ideal for working in two colours, which can create very pretty effects. When using two colours, work all large crosses first, followed by the additional stitches in the second colour. Rice stitch is worked over an even number of threads, usually over four threads of an evenweave fabric but it can also be worked to occupy the space of four blocks of Aida. Do not pull the stitch and form holes around the edge.

✕✕✕✕✕

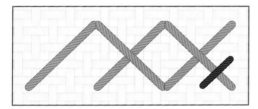

1 *Rice stitch is formed by starting to the left of a vertical thread, working a half cross stitch across four evenweave threads, returning to complete the cross. By the third stage of Fig 1 additional stitches have been added in a second colour.*

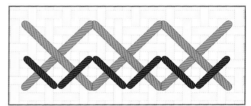

2 *The additional stitches across the legs are traditionally worked as a back stitch into the central side hole in each case.*

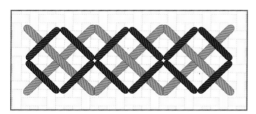

3 *Three completed rice stitches. To ensure uniformity across a project, remember in which direction you stitched, and do all the additional stitches in the same way.*

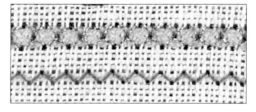

In this section of the Spring Sampler, rice stitch has been stitched in a single colour with metallic gold added as a second colour.

Diagonal Rice Stitch

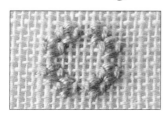

For an interesting variation rice stitch can be worked diagonally, in which case the stitch appears vertically.

Diagonal rice stitch is very effective worked in two colours.

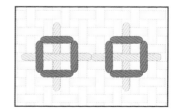

Tent Stitch

Also known as continental tent stitch

Tent stitch is best known as a canvaswork stitch. It has long slanting stitches on the back and even, full stitches on the front. It is the long slanting stitches on the back which cause the distortion of the canvas which is characteristic of this stitch. Tent stitch is sometimes mistaken for half cross stitch but it uses a third more wool than half cross stitch and creates a much thicker and harder-wearing stitch, which makes it ideal for furnishings.

✗✗✗✗✗

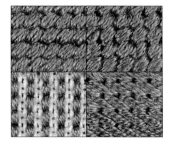

Top left: half cross stitch.
Bottom left: the back of half cross stitch.
Top right: tent stitch.
Bottom right: the back of tent stitch.

Tent stitch is a diagonal stitch formed by the needle being taken under the stitches from right to left thus supporting the stitches, using more thread and so forming a fuller stitch. Ensure that you don't use tent stitch in one direction and half cross stitch in the other. This gives the work the appearance of a furrowed field and is very disappointing.

Diagonal Tent Stitch

The alternative name for diagonal tent stitch is basketweave stitch because of the woven effect produced on the reverse.

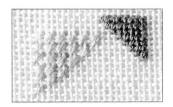

Diagonal tent stitch worked over one thread (right) and two threads (left).

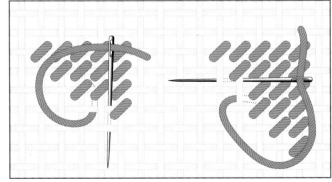

The stitches used in diagonal tent stitch are worked diagonally across the canvas threads so they distort the canvas less than ordinary tent stitch. This method produces a full, even stitch and is pleasing to work. It is a good idea to use straight lines of tent stitch for working a design and then complete the background in diagonal tent stitch.

Gobelin Stitch

Gobelin stitch is a straight stitch often used as a filling stitch as it can mimic the appearance of a woven tapestry. The stitch can be worked to form regular shapes or be worked in encroaching rows to create softer shapes. It can also be worked as long stitches in zigzag rows to form the Florentine pattern. When worked as Florentine or flame stitch, the work created is often known as bargello and is used as a hard-wearing stitch for upholstery.

Gobelin stitch can be worked in stranded cotton or in crewel or tapestry wool and should not be pulled too tight.

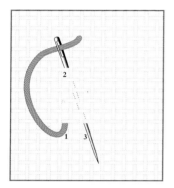

1 Work a long, straight stitch over the number of threads indicated on the chart following the numbered sequence in the diagram. The stitch should lie flat and not pull or distort the fabric.

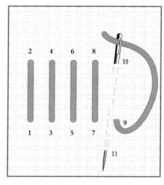

2 Leaving a space for the second row, work along the row positioning the needle to return to fill the gaps.

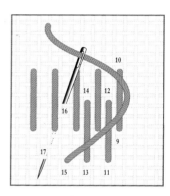

3 Continuing to follow the numbered sequence in the diagram, work the second row of stitches which should encroach on the first row.

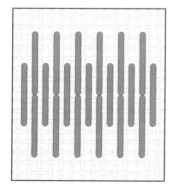

4 This diagram shows the way a third row of straight stitches fits the space.

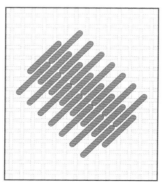

The same stitching principles apply when working a slanted version of gobelin stitch.

The two heart motifs on this page show the effect that may be created when different colours are used for gobelin stitch. The top version of the heart is worked in one colour while the same motif stitched below illustrates a Florentine pattern as used in bargello.

Satin Stitch

Also known as damask stitch

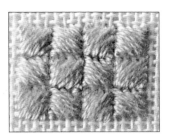

This is a long, smooth stitch which covers the fabric and is often used to fill in shapes. When worked in a glossy thread like stranded cotton (floss), the stitch should have a velvety sheen and can look very effective when worked in blocks facing in different directions. Avoid using very long lengths of thread as this will suffer by being pulled through the fabric too many times. You may like to experiment with the number of strands of thread used, to vary the effect – many strands can give an almost padded look.

✕✕✕✕✕

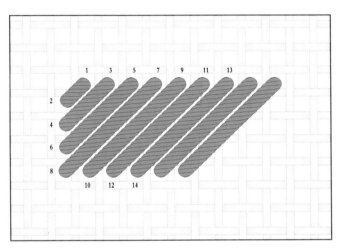

To work satin stitch, start a thread with an away waste knot (see page 18) rather than the loop method which reverses the twist on the thread. Beginning to the left of a vertical thread, follow the numbered sequence in the diagram, laying flat stitches side by side. Always come up the same side and down the other side, so that the back of the fabric is covered. In this way, the stitches will lie closely and neatly beside each other. Take care not to pull satin stitch too tight; it is not intended to distort the fabric. It can be worked diagonally as shown, horizontally or vertically.

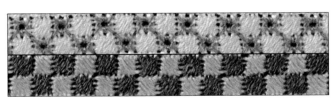

Satin stitch can be worked in the same direction or in a checkerboard style. The shaded effect created by changing direction gives the illusion that two colours have been used.

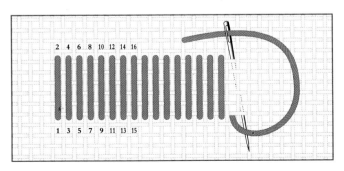

Satin stitch worked vertically.

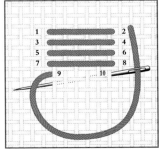

Satin stitch worked horizontally.

❋ The Summer Sampler ❋

Stitch Count: 90 x 169

Design Size: 16.5 x 31cm (6½ x 12¼in)

Fabric Selection: Ivory or antique white linen 28 threads to 2.5cm (1in)

Tapestry Needle Size: 26 and 22

This is the second seasonal sampler. It is worked as a band sampler and the stitches needed are described on the chart on pages 169–171 and include cross stitch, back stitch and a number of more unusual counted stitches, pulled thread work and Hardanger embroidery. All the stitches in this sampler are included in the Stitch Library but I recommend that you also read Pulled and Drawn Thread Work and Hardanger Embroidery (pages 66 and 70) before starting to stitch.

The chart is over three pages with no over-lapping. You might find it easiest to photocopy the parts and tape them together.

Using stranded cottons (floss) unless other-wise stated, work the cross stitch first, followed by the additional counted stitches and then the Hardanger and other pulled or drawn stitches. Refer to the Stitch Library for the stitch diagrams and relevant instructions as you need them.

Work the Bands as follows:
- Use two strands of stranded cotton for the full and three-quarter cross stitches, double cross stitch, Algerian eye, French knots, queen stitch and Rhodes stitch.
- Use three strands of stranded cotton (floss) for the satin stitch.

- Add back stitch outline where required, using one strand of the colour indicated on the chart.
- Add the random French knots in dark pink stranded cotton (floss) to the large individual strawberries after completing the cross stitch.
- When working the Algerian eyes, remember to keep the working thread away from the small hole in the centre of the stitch. *Always* form the stitch by passing the needle *down* the centre hole each time.
- Use one strand of gold metallic thread where indicated on the chart (see page 46 for tips and hints on using metallics).

Work the Hardanger as follows:
- Work the Kloster blocks using one strand of ecru perlé cotton No. 5, counting over four threads of the linen. Keep checking that the blocks are directly opposite each other, refer-ring to the diagrams on page 71 as necessary.
- When all the Kloster blocks are complete, use very sharp, pointed scissors to cut across the ends of the blocks. Take this section slowly, counting and cutting four threads each time.
- Needleweave the remaining linen threads using one strand of ecru perlé cotton No. 8, adding the dove's eye stitches as you needleweave, as indicated on the chart.

Back Stitch

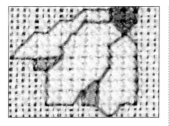

Back stitch is used for creating an outline around a design or part of a design, to add detail or emphasis. The addition of a back stitch outline to a counted cross stitch pattern is a modern idea and in some cases excessive outlining is used to disguise rather poor design so it should be treated with caution. It is not always necessary and is often a matter of taste. On a chart, back stitch is usually indicated by solid lines surrounding the symbols with the suggested shade indicated on the chart or in the key. It is added after the cross stitch has been completed, to prevent the back stitch line being broken by the cross stitches. Try to use a shade of thread for the back stitch that defines the cross stitch but avoid black unless it is specifically required (e.g. for wrought iron railings).

Another important use of back stitch is for lettering and numerals, allowing you to stitch verses, messages, dates and so on and thus personalise your work. You may like to experiment with different back stitch alphabets, thread colours and the number of strands of cotton (floss) used. Refer to page 21 for tips on working back stitch outlining.

✕✕✕✕✕

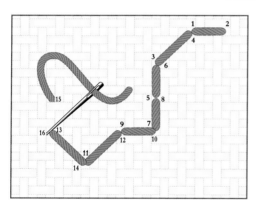

To work back stitches, follow the numbered sequence shown in the diagram, working the stitches over one block of Aida or over two threads of evenweave, unless stated otherwise on the chart. Long loose stitches may be used for ship rigging, cat's whiskers and so on.

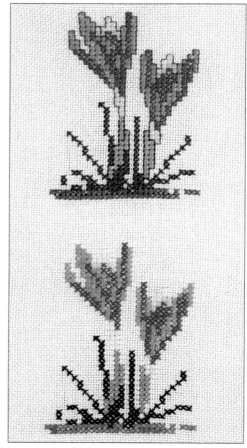

This simple but effective crocus motif has been stitched using two techniques but on the same fabric. The top version has been stitched in two strands of stranded cotton (floss) and back stitch outlined in one strand. The outline colour has been taken from the colours used for the cross stitch to ensure a soft, realistic look. The second version, worked from the same chart, has been stitched using one strand of German Flower Thread and the back stitch outline has been omitted. You can see that both techniques are effective but create quite a different feel.

Double Running Stitch
Also known as Holbein stitch

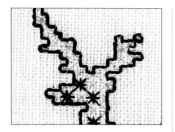

This ancient deer pattern has been embellished with black and metallic gold double running stitch.

Double running or Holbein stitch is the traditional stitch for creating blackwork patterns because the stitch should look the same on the back and front of the work. If back stitch is used instead of double running stitch it creates a rather padded and untidy reverse. The stitch should be created in two jour–neys, working alternate stitches and then returning to fill the gaps created. The photograph below shows a modern holly and berry motif worked in double running stitch, using green and red stranded cotton (floss). When working blackwork patterns using double running stitch, you need to plan your stitching route so that you can complete all the stitches on the return journey. See page 60 for further advice on blackwork.

×××××

1 To work double running stitch, first work a running stitch, counting to ensure that you work under and over two threads of evenweave or one block of Aida in each case.

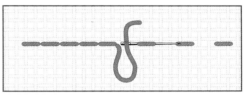

2 Follow the second part of the diagram to fill in the gaps on the return journey, making the stitch truly reversible.

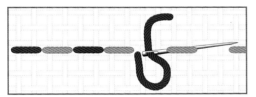

Double running stitch can be worked in two colours by simply changing colour before completing the gaps on the return journey.

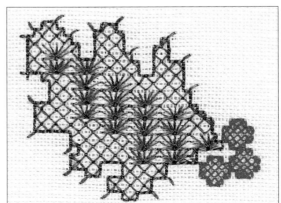

A simple but decorative holly motif created by working the outline first and then filling in with blackwork patterns.

Montenegrin Stitch

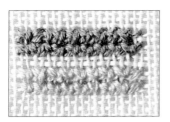

This unusual stitch looks similar to long-legged cross stitch but is constructed in a different way and includes an extra vertical leg which gives it a richer and fuller appearance. The stitch, although not truly reversible, is neat and consistent on the back. It can also be worked on Aida fabric by moving two blocks forward and one block up.

This stitch forms an embossed braid on the front of the stitching and makes a fine, raised edge for folding.

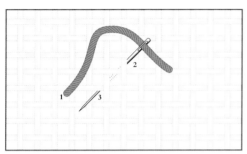

1 To work Montenegrin stitch on evenweave fabric start to the left of a vertical thread. Following the numbered sequence, work a long diagonal 'leg' by moving four threads forwards and two threads up. Bring the needle two threads back and two threads down to emerge at 3.

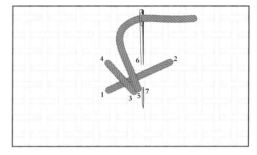

2 Insert the needle two threads backwards diagonally to make the short leg at 4. Bring the needle back up at 5 and down at 6 to form the final vertical leg.

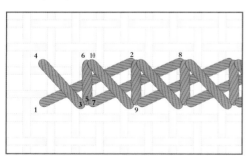

This diagram shows the pattern created by repeating Montenegrin stitch.

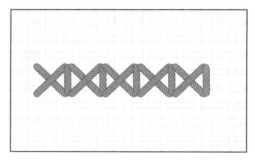

How the back of the work should look after several Montenegrin stitches.

This detail from the Autumn Sampler on page 108 illustrates two rows of Montenegrin stitch in two colours forming a frame for the hem stitched area.

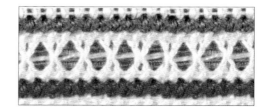

Counted Chain Stitch

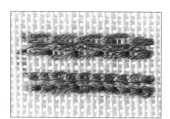

Counted chain stitch is very versatile as it may be used on Aida or evenweave fabric as part of a pattern or to join sections of stitching together. It can be used as an outline stitch or worked in close rows when filling in a pattern.

If using counted chain stitch to join sections of stitching you normally use the same colour thread for the join or you could use a contrasting colour, shown in the photograph below (this clearly illustrates the join).

✗✗✗✗✗

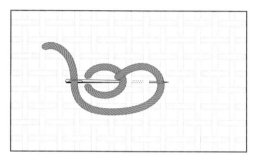

1 *To work chain stitch, start to the left of a vertical thread, bring the needle through the fabric and back down the same hole forming a loop on the surface. Pass the point of the needle under two threads and up to the surface forming another loop. Each new stitch thus anchors the previous stitch and so on.*

2 *If chain stitch is worked as a border the last stitch will anchor the first one. If not, the last and first stitch may be anchored over one thread as shown here.*

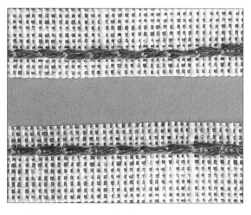

1 *To join two pieces of work, stitch a row of counted chain stitch along the edges of the two pieces. Fold in raw edges and work chain stitch lines side by side.*

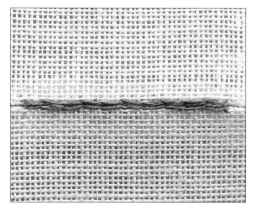

2 *Using the same or contrasting thread, weave in and out of the chain stitch to form a pretty join.*

Stem Stitch

Stem stitch is another surface embroidery stitch I have borrowed with success. The secret is to form the stitch in the same manner for the whole project, carefully counting the threads each time. Using spare fabric, experiment with turning gentle corners to perfect your technique. The stitch is most effective on evenweave fabric.

✕✕✕✕✕

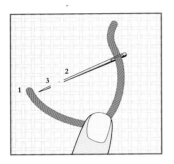 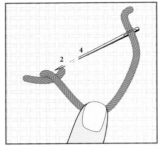 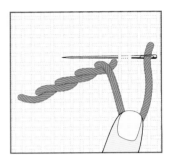

1 *To work stem stitch, follow the numbered sequence in the diagram, working a straight stitch across four threads on evenweave, passing the needle back two threads.*

2 *Make the next stitch by holding the thread over and below the previous stitch and working across four threads again.*

3 *Repeat the stitching sequence so each stitch is formed in the same manner, checking that each new stitch is on the same side to create the rope-like effect required.*

Herringbone Stitch

Also known as plaited stitch, catch stitch, fishnet stitch and witch stitch

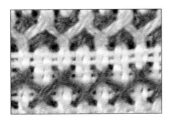

This simple and decorative stitch is often used on band samplers, making it a fine companion to cross stitch and it looks particularly pretty when combined with stitches like long-legged cross stitch. It can also be whipped with a second colour. It is shown here worked over four evenweave threads diagonally and under two horizontally. It can be worked over two and under one to make it smaller, or over and under more threads to make it larger.

✕✕✕✕✕

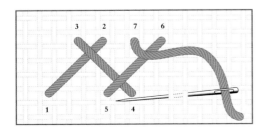

Herringbone stitch is formed starting to the left of a vertical thread, across the number of threads indicated on the chart, following the numbered sequence shown in the diagram.

Algerian Eye

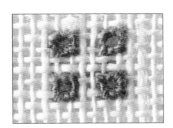

This pretty star-shaped stitch is a pulled stitch which means that when formed correctly holes are pulled in the fabric. It usually occupies the space taken by four cross stitches. It is an ideal stitch to combine with cross stitch as it can add a delicate lacy appearance without the anxiety of cutting threads. Algerian eye can be worked over two or four threads of evenweave as shown and is more successful worked on evenweave than Aida. (See also eyelet variations overleaf.)

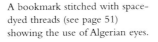

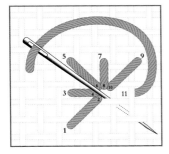

1 *To work an Algerian eye, start to the left of a vertical thread and work from left to right around each stitch in an anticlockwise direction (or vice versa but keeping each stitch the same).*

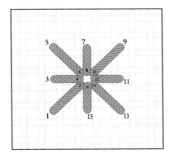

2 *Always work the stitch by passing the needle down through the central hole, as shown in the diagram, pulling quite firmly so that a small hole is formed in the centre. Take care that trailing threads do not cover this hole as you progress to the next stitch.*

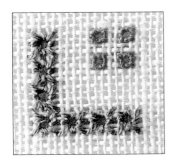

This shows that Algerian eye may be stitched over one or two threads very effectively.

Algerian eye worked over only two evenweave threads.

A bookmark stitched with space-dyed threads (see page 51) showing the use of Algerian eyes.

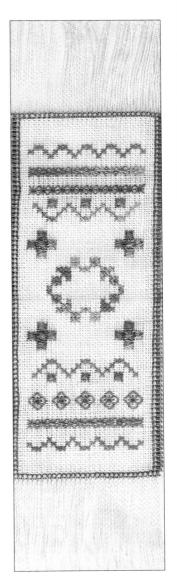

Eyelet Variations

There are a number of eyelet stitch variations, some of which are shown in the diagrams and photograph here. You can choose the shape you like and work it over more or less threads to create larger or smaller eyelets.

The rules are the same for all eyelets. As with the Algerian eye you need to work the stitch in the correct order and in one direction to ensure that the hole created is uniform and as round as possible. When following the numbered sequence on the diagrams always work the stitch by passing the needle down through the central hole each time, and take care that trailing threads do not cover this hole as you progress to the next stitch.

Why not try inventing eyelet stitches of your own? Work the stitch in the correct sequence and always pass the needle down the central hole, and see what effects you can create.

✕✕✕✕✕

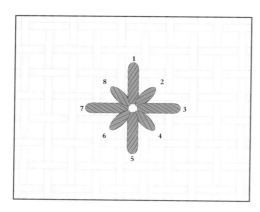

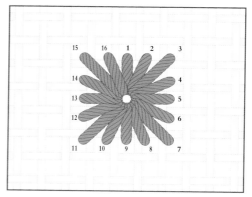

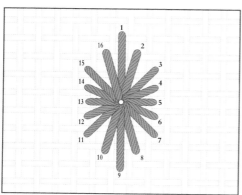

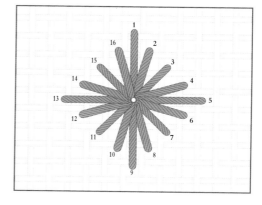

Queen Stitch

Also known as Rococo stitch

This is an ancient pulled stitch made of four parts and forming little dimples in the embroidery by pulling small holes in the fabric. Although this stitch looks fairly unexciting on its own it is gorgeous when worked as a group. As it is a fairly labour-intensive stitch it is best used in small areas like the strawberry detail, left, from the Summer Band Sampler shown on page 98.

Following the instructions and diagrams, work the stitch over a square of four threads in four stages. This stitch is traditionally worked from right to left, but if you find this difficult to count, try working the two middle parts first followed by the outer ones.

✕✕✕✕✕

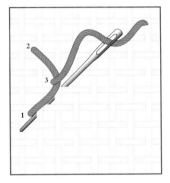

1 *Work one long stitch over four threads of the fabric which is then moved two threads to the right by the needle coming up at 3 and a small stitch worked across one thread.*

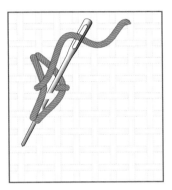

2 *Repeat the long stitch from the same position as in fig 1, but this time bending the stitch over one thread only.*

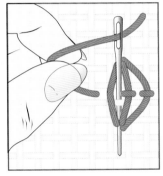

3 *Repeat the long stitch from the same position as in fig 1, but this time the long stitch is bent to the left and the needle re-enters the fabric in the centre position.*

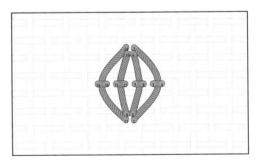

4 *The last stage of the stitch is completed forming a lantern shape on the fabric. Note how the top and bottom hole is shared by each stage of the stitch so forming the holes or little dimples that make this stitch distinctive.*

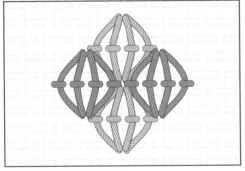

5 *You can work Queen stitch individually or in groups. Notice how the stitches are 'joined' together - they may be outlined with back stitch if preferred.*

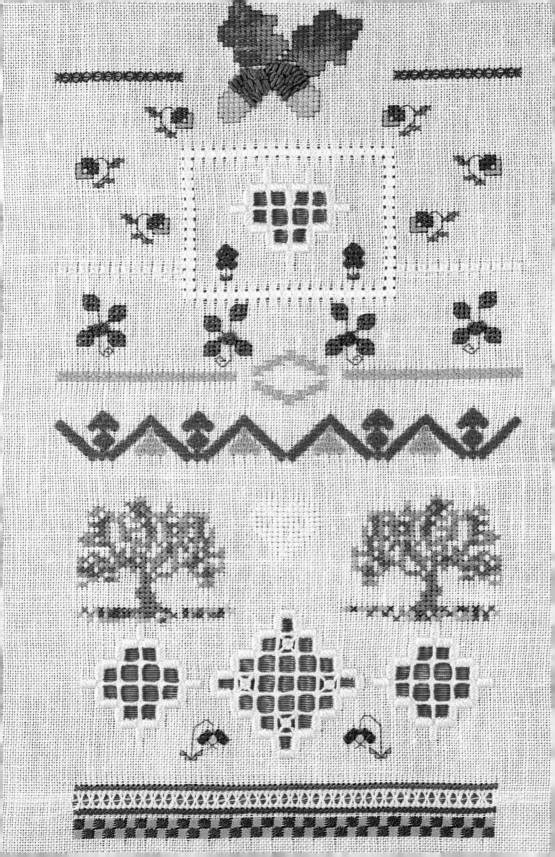

✻ The Autumn Sampler ✻

Stitch Count: 83 x 166
Design Size: 15 x 30cm (6 x 12in)
Fabric Selection: Zweigart Cashel linen 28 threads to 2.5cm (1in)
Tapestry Needle Size: 24–22

This is the third seasonal sampler. It is worked as a band sampler and the stitches needed are described on the chart on pages 172-174 and include cross stitch, back stitch and a number of more unusual counted stitches, pulled thread work and Hardanger embroidery. All the stitches in this sampler are included in the Stitch Library but I recommend that you also read Pulled and Drawn Thread Work and Hardanger Embroidery (pages 66 and 70) before starting to stitch.

The chart is over three pages with no overlapping. You might find it easiest to photocopy the parts and tape them together.

Using stranded cottons (floss) unless otherwise stated, work the cross stitch first, followed by the additional counted stitches and then the Hardanger and other pulled or drawn stitches. Refer to the Stitch Library for the stitch diagrams and relevant instructions as you need them.

Work the Bands as follows:
- Use two strands of stranded cotton for the cross stitch, double cross stitch, rice stitch, French knots, half Rhodes stitch with bar, queen stitch, Montenegrin stitch, four-sided stitch and bullion knots.
- Add back stitch outline where required, using one strand of the colour indicated on the chart.
- Use three strands of stranded cotton (floss) for the satin stitch.
- When working the bullion bars, use a size 22 needle to create full but straight stitches. This is a good opportunity for tweeding, using a mixture

of autumn colours such as 940, 920 and 976.
- For the French knot clusters, tweed the threads to mix the colours (see page 14) and work the stitches at random piling them in groups as shown.
- Where the rice stitch is worked in two colours, work the large cross over *four* threads in two strands of stranded cotton (floss) and add the small stitches in *one* strand of gold metallic.
- Work one row of four-sided stitch around the square as shown on the chart, but work over *four* threads instead of two.
- For the tied hem stitch, work two rows of hem stitch following the chart. Working from the centre of the hem-stitched box, carefully snip each horizontal linen thread down the centre line once and using a needle, un-pick the linen threads back to the two outside edges and carefully weave the threads into the fabric thus forming a selvedge. You should be left with vertical threads only. Referring to the diagrams on page 114, work one row of tied hem stitch.

Work the Hardanger as follows:
- Work the Kloster blocks using one strand of perlé cotton No. 5 counting over four threads of the linen. Keep checking that the blocks are directly opposite each other, referring to the diagrams as necessary.
- When all the Kloster blocks are complete, use very sharp, pointed scissors to cut across the ends of the blocks. Take this section slowly, counting and cutting two threads each time.
- Needleweave the remaining linen threads using one strand of perlé cotton No. 8, adding spider's web filling stitch as indicated.

Four-Sided Stitch

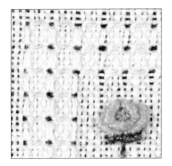

Four-sided stitch is traditionally worked as a pulled stitch to create a lacy effect without the removal of threads from the fabric. It can also be used as a hem stitch when threads are to be cut or removed.

The secret of creating four-sided stitch correctly is to make sure that your needle travels in the correct direction on the back of the stitch. The stitches on the front of your work should be vertical or horizontal whilst on the back they should be diagonal. It is this tension which forms the small holes as the stitch is worked. It is possible to work four-sided stitch on Aida fabric but is not recommended.

✕✕✕✕✕

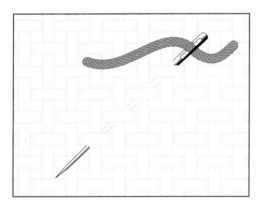

1 *To work four-sided stitch, begin to the left of a vertical thread and work a horizontal straight stitch across four threads (or the number indicated on the chart), passing the needle diagonally across four threads at the back of the work.*

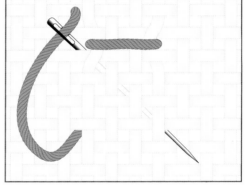

2 *Bring the needle up and form a vertical straight stitch, again passing the needle diagonally across four threads at the back of the work.*

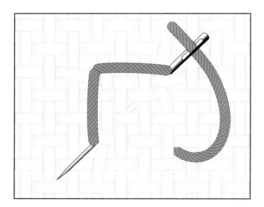

3 *Bring the needle up and form another vertical straight stitch, again passing the needle diagonally across four threads at the back.*

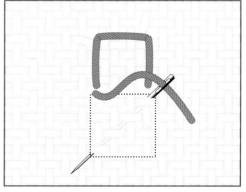

4 *Work a horizontal straight stitch to form the last side of the square but this time pass the needle across diagonally to begin the next stitch.*

Hem Stitch

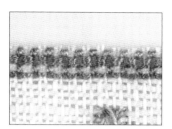

When working hem stitches for the first time it is simple to work them without removing any threads, eliminating the anxiety of cutting too many! When you have perfected the stitch you can experiment with thread removal. As you can see from the diagrams the stitch is made up of parts, two straight stitches and one diagonal on the back. It is this combination which forms the safe barrier if threads are to be cut or removed. If you are intending to cut to the edge, you may prefer to use double hem stitch as described overleaf. Hem stitch can look very effective worked in rows without any threads removed. This stitch is not suitable for Aida.

✕ ✕ ✕ ✕ ✕

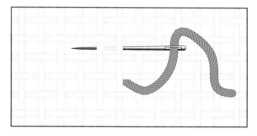

1 *This shows hem stitching over two threads in each direction. Work a straight stitch across two threads, turning the needle to face horizontally.*

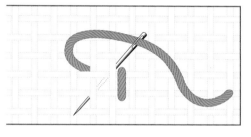

2 *Make another straight stitch across two threads, at right angles to the first stitch, then pass the needle down diagonally under two threads.*

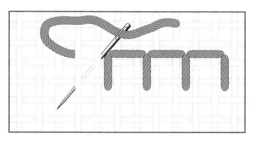

3 *Repeat the straight stitches along the row, counting carefully.*

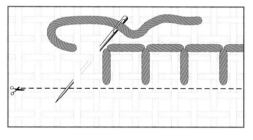

4 *After the hem stitching is complete, the threads indicated may be cut away.*

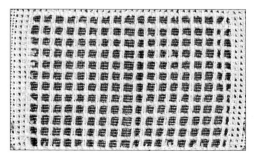

This detail from the Spring Sampler on page 90 illustrates two rows of hem stitching.

Double Hem Stitch

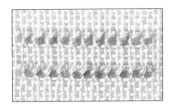

This stitch is formed in the same manner as single hem stitch but worked twice. If you intend to cut to the edge of the stitching and are nervous about it, work the stitches first, pull one thread out adjacent to the stitches and then cut away any excess. The needle should be straight on the front of the work, diagonal on the back. Both single and double hem stitch are usually worked in the same shade as the fabric.

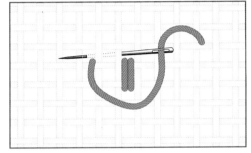

1 *This diagram shows double hem stitching over two threads in each direction. Work two vertical stitches across two threads, turning the needle to face horizontally.*

2 *Work across two threads passing the needle across horizontally under the two threads. Work this stitch twice and note the stitches share entry and exit points.*

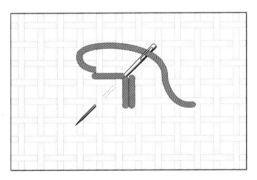

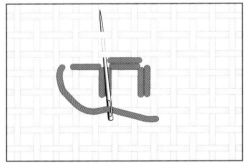

3 *Pass the needle diagonally across the two threads prior to repeating the stitch. Repeat the straight and diagonal stitches along the row counting carefully and checking that the needle travels diagonally at the back of the work.*

4 *This diagram shows how to turn a corner neatly whilst hem stitching.*

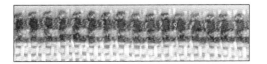

The edge of the space-dyed bookmark (see page 51) showing double hem stitch.

Hem Stitch Variations

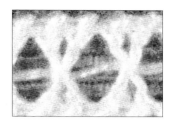

This exquisite group of decorative filling stitches are formed on the remaining vertical threads after hem stitching and thread withdrawal. When working the stitches described here, it is important to refer also to the descriptions of Pulled and Drawn Thread (page 66) and Hem Stitching (page 68). With dozens of filling styles used for decorating and strengthening the remaining threads after thread withdrawal, I can only show a few examples here.

✕✕✕✕✕

Somersault Stitch

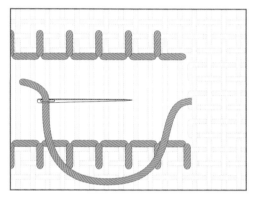

1 *To work a row of somersault stitches on groups of two threads within a hem-stitched frame, first remove the number of fabric threads indicated on the chart you are following. Start with a waste knot and bring the needle up where indicated.*

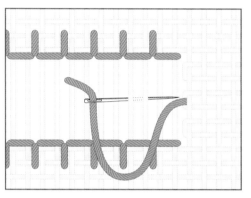

2 *Count four fabric threads and insert the needle under two threads amd up between the two pairs, so the needle is positioned over the second pair of threads. Don't pull the needle through the work yet.*

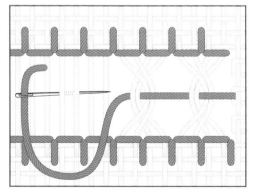

3 *Without removing the needle from these threads, twist the needle until it faces the other way. The threads will twist automatically as you do this.*

4 *Pinch your fingers together over this stitch and gently pull the needle through, keeping the thread horizontal and taut. Repeat this process down the row, fastening off into the fabric edge.*

Double Somersault Stitch

Double somersault stitch is worked in exactly the same way as normal somersault stitch, creating a wonderfully decorative look. It may be worked across large areas of withdrawn threads although it is difficult to keep the lines neat when more than one row is worked.

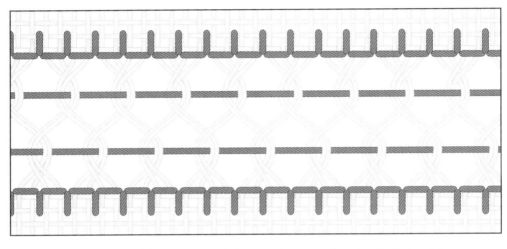

Double somersault stitch has two rows worked on opposite groups of two threads. Perfect stitches should be evenly worked and the lines between the stitches should be as straight as possible.

Tied Hem Stitch

This pretty but very simple hem stitch variation is created by hem stitching two rows, withdrawing the intervening threads and then simply using the needle to tie groups of threads together as shown in the diagrams. Keep the knotted lines as straight as you can.

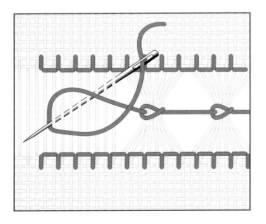

1 *Begin in the same way as somersault stitch, then take the needle and thread over a group of four threads, knotting them around as shown.*

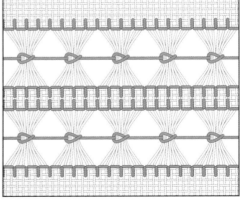

2 *The secret of perfection is to ensure that the tying thread is as straight as possible.*

Buttonhole Stitch

The buttonhole stitches illustrated here are included to allow you to produce projects like the Hardanger coaster heart (shown right and described on page 73). The cross stitch and Hardanger embroidery is completed, then buttonhole stitches are worked around the perimeter so the shape can be cut out without fear of the design falling to pieces!

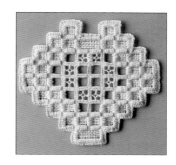

✕✕✕✕✕

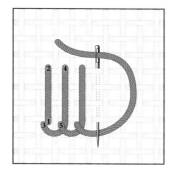

To work buttonhole stitch, start with an away waste knot (see page 18) and work long stitches over four threads (similar to Kloster blocks).

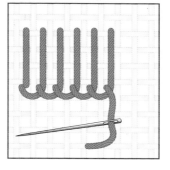

Keep the stitches flat against the fabric and as consistent as possible.

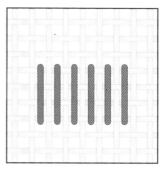

This shows what the stitching should look like at the back.

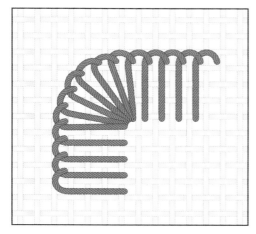

When you turn outer corners in buttonhole stitch, note that the corner hole holds seven threads.

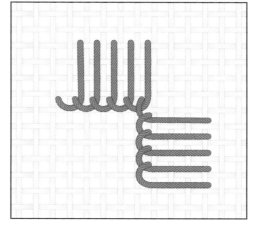

When turning internal corners, note the way the corner stitches are connected.

French Knot

French knots are small but very important stitches but probably cause more distress than any other stitch as they can disappear to the back of the work or worse still, end up as a row of tiny knots on the thread in the needle. They are often crucial to a design as probably their most common use is adding tiny eyes to cross stitched faces.

✕✕✕✕✕

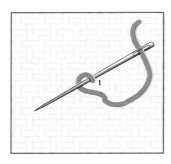

1 *To work a French knot, bring the needle through to the front of the fabric and wind the thread around the needle twice.*

2 *Begin to 'post' the needle partly through to the back, one thread or part of a block away from the entry point. (This will stop the stitch being pulled to the wrong side.)*

3 *Gently pull the thread you have wound so that it sits snugly at the point where the needle enters the fabric. Pull the needle through to the back and you should have a perfect knot in position. If you want bigger knots, add more thread to the needle as this gives a better result than winding more times round the needle.*

Palestrina Knot

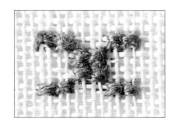

A palestrina knot (see the detail left and the photograph of the decorative thistle on page 116) is a truly counted stitch and is ideal when a uniform and carefully centred stitch is needed. With the best will in the world, French knots do have a habit of wandering on the surface of the fabric whereas a palestrina knot is centred on the square. It can be formed on Aida or even-weave. It takes a little practice so try it on a spare piece of fabric.

✕✕✕✕✕

❋ *Decorative Thistle* ❋

Stitch Count: 56 x 86
Design Size: 10 x 16cm
(4 x 6¼in)
Fabric Selection: Grey Jobelan
27/28 threads to 2.5cm (1in)
Tapestry Needle Size: 24

This gorgeous thistle design (left) was stitched using stranded cotton (floss) and stranded metallic gold thread. The flower head was outlined in back stitch worked from the chart on page 147 and then completely filled in using random French knots and tiny glass beads (from Beadesign – see Suppliers). The stem and leaves are worked in cross stitch with a little back stitch outline. The corner border motifs are worked in a combination of palestrina knots and cross stitch. See Working the Projects page 126.

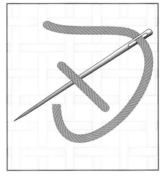

1 *A palestrina knot is formed on the surface of the fabric and occupies the same space as one cross stitch. Start to the left of a vertical thread and form a half cross stitch. Instead of completing the cross stitch, pass the needle under the diagonal stitch to form a loop, keeping the leading thread fairly taut.*

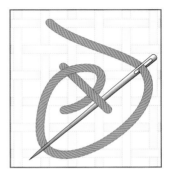

2 *Pass the needle under the diagonal stitch, again forming a second loop and pulling the knot formed firmly.*

3 *Pass the needle down through the fabric in the place indicated in the diagram to complete the square.*

4 *When the stitch is complete, a palestrina knot should look rather like a cross stitch with a full bar across it.*

Bullion Stitch

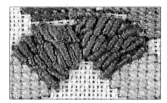

This unusual stitch is not a counted stitch but can add a three-dimensional texture to a design. It can be formed in straight lines, adapted to make a raised bar, and can also be made to curve for petal shapes and for building up roses (see below). Bullion bars are easier to form using a gold-plated needle! Don't panic when you reach fig 4 – careful teasing with a needle will rescue the apparent disaster.

✕✕✕✕✕

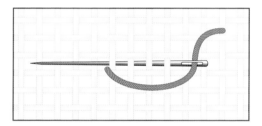

1 *To work a straight bullion stitch or bar, start with a back stitch the same length and in the same position as you want the finished bar to be. Do not complete the back stitch but leave the needle in the fabric. It is vital that the point of the needle exits from the hole where it started.*

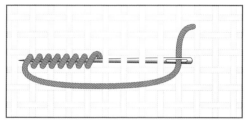

2 *Wind the thread round the needle as many times as necessary to make the coil the intended length of the finished bar.*

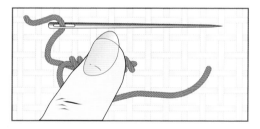

3 *Hold the needle and its coil of thread firmly against the fabric with your thumb, then gently but firmly pull the needle through the coil and the fabric.*

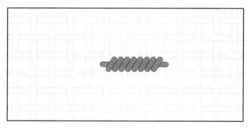

4 *Turn the coil back on itself and push the needle through the fabric at the rear of the back stitch. If necessary, hold the thread firmly at the back of the fabric and tease the bullion stitch into shape.*

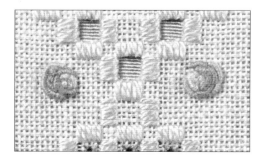

To work bullion bars for the roses in the Bow Band Sampler on page 6, start in the same way as described above in Figs 1 and 2 but wind the thread around the needle more times; these added threads will force the stitch to curl when complete. Roses may be formed by working different lengths of curved bullion bars and by using a number of colours. As can be seen in the photograph, the rose was formed by working three French knots and then placing bullion bars around them, anchoring them into position if necessary.

❋ Framed Canvas Stitch Sampler and ❋ Canvas Stitch Scissors Keeper

Stitch Count: 31 x 31
Design Size: 6 x 6cm (2¹/₄ x 2¹/₄in)
Fabric Selection: Grey Jobelan 27/28 threads to 2.5cm (1in)
Tapestry Needle Size: 22

These two designs are by Sue Hawkins, author, designer and Technical Director of the Cross Stitch Guild. Both are stitched on 14-count single canvas using three strands of Appleton crewel wool over one thread of canvas. The sampler includes Rhodes stitch, tent stitch, satin stitch and long-legged cross stitch and is charted on page 152. To work the sampler, complete the four textured squares as on the chart, then work around the edge with long-legged cross stitch. Add one or two rows of tent stitch as necessary to fill the aperture of your frame so no unstitched canvas shows.

The scissors keeper is not charted but shows what can be achieved by mixing stitches. It includes queen stitch, long-legged cross stitch, tent stitch, French knots, rice stitch and vertical double cross stitch. It has been made up with a twisted cord and a tassel (see page 186).

Wrapped Bars and Spider's Webs

When working the stitches described here, it is important to refer back to the Hardanger Embroidery section (page 70), where all the principles and techniques are described in more detail. The description of these stitches is merely an introduction to the fun that can be had combining them with cross stitch.

After Kloster blocks have been formed (see page 70/71) and the threads have been cut and removed (see page 72) the four remaining threads are reinforced in a decorative fashion using wrapping or needleweaving. Additional decorative elements may be added whilst this is being stitched, such as spider's web stitch with wrapped bars and picots with needleweaving (see page 122).

Needleweaving or wrapping is traditionally done with a finer perlé cotton than that used for stitching the Kloster blocks. Needleweaving (see page 74) involves the thread being woven over and under the threads that remain after cutting. Wrapping bars simply means that the thread is wound around and around two or four threads after cutting. To work these stitches, follow the sequence in the diagrams, ensuring that you work each section in the same manner, counting the wraps or weaves.

×××××

Wrapped Bars

Wrapped bars may be worked alone to decorate the threads that remain after cutting, or as part of other decorative stitches, such as spider's webs shown opposite. As you wrap each bar you will need to hold the threads you are wrapping quite firmly to prevent them from unravelling as you work. It does take a little practise before your wrapped bars look perfect.

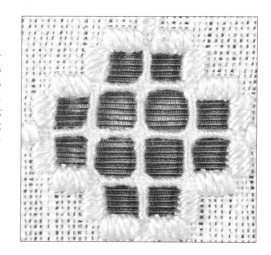

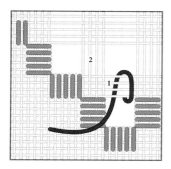

1 *Start by anchoring the thread under adjacent Kloster blocks and begin wrapping from a cut area.*

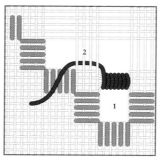

2 *Wind the thread around and around the four threads as shown, then travel to the next group of threads.*

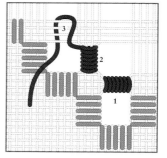

3 *Continue wrapping the bars around as shown, keeping a check on how many times each set is wrapped and keeping all the stitches consistent.*

Spider's Web Stitch

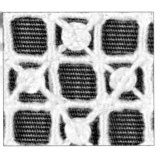

Spider's web is a traditional filling stitch used to decorate the voids left by cutting threads and it is often used with wrapped bars. As with all these stitches although they are not counted it is a good idea to keep notes of numbers of winds and weaves to ensure the stitches are uniform.

✗✗✗✗✗

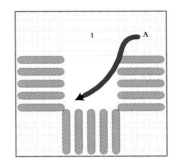

1 *Work three sides in Kloster blocks, wrapped bars or a combination of both as seen here, bringing the needle out at A.*

2 *Cross the square, bringing the needle out at B.*

3 *Return to A, winding the thread around the diagonal just formed, ready to complete the final side, shown as a wrapped bar in fig 4.*

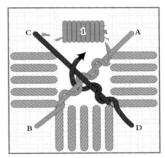

4 *Bring the needle up at C and pass diagonally to D, then wind the thread around the diagonal to the centre (as shown in step 3).*

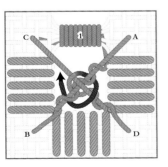

5 *Start weaving the spider's web around the diagonals as shown.*

6 *After three winds you may need to tighten and adjust the position of the winds to ensure they are even and in the centre of the square.*

7 *When the web is complete, leave the stitch by winding around the diagonal as before.*

Needleweaving, Picots and Dove's Eyes

Needleweaving

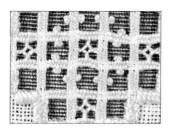

Needleweaving is used on the loose threads that are left when stitched Kloster blocks have been cut, especially over large areas. The needleweaving creates covered bars, and the spaces between the bars can be filled with decorative stitches such as dove's eye (see opposite). The bars themselves can also be decorated with stitches such as picots (see opposite). When working the stitches described here, it is important to refer back to the section on Hardanger (page 70).

✕✕✕✕✕

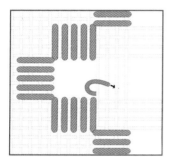

1 *To needleweave, start by anchoring the thread under adjacent Kloster blocks on the reverse of the work.*

2 *Beginning from a cut area, bring the needle up through a void area.*

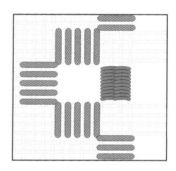

3 *Weave the needle under and over pairs of threads to form a plaited effect. These stitches should not distort or bend the threads.*

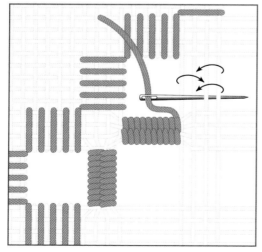

4 *After completing one bar, weave the next one at right angles to it, working around the design and taking care not to run threads across the back of the cut area.*

This shows a detail of some of the needleweaving in the Hardanger Flower Needlecase shown on page 75.

Picots

These pretty, decorative elements are worked as you wrap or needleweave the remaining threads after cutting, taking care to work each section in a uniform style. It will take a little practise to perfect these stitches but when worked they are very effective.

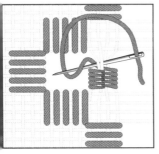
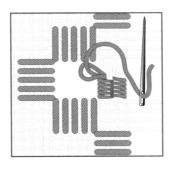
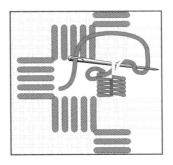

1 *After cutting the threads, needleweave halfway along a set of four threads as described in needleweaving on page 122. Bring the needle out at the side to form the picot. Pass the needle under two threads on the same side and wrap the thread around the needle as shown.*

2 *Pull the needle through carefully, holding the wrapped thread in position. Do not pull too tightly. Pass the needle through the centre of the four fabric threads, ready to make another picot along the other edge in the same way.*

3 *Once both picots have been formed the needleweaving can be completed. Keep a record of how many weaves you make either side of the picots with the aim of keeping all the stitches consistent.*

Dove's Eye Stitch

Dove's eye stitch is a traditional Hardanger stitch which is constructed whilst needleweaving. It is possible to add it as an afterthought but this is not recommended. The stitch should be with the diamond-shaped hole forming in the centre of the void left by cutting. This may take practice and need a 'little pinching and pulling' to achieve perfect results. Refer also to the Hardanger section starting on page 70.

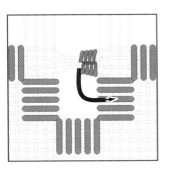
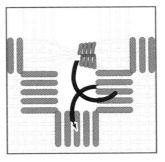
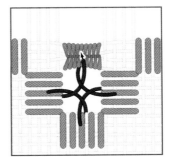

1 *Whilst working the last side of a square, needleweave to the centre of the bar, bringing the needle out through the void area.*

2 *Pierce the neighbouring Kloster block or needlewoven bar halfway along its length, bringing the needle up through the void and through the loop formed by the thread.*

3 *Continue around the square following the sequence in the diagram, but before resuming the needleweaving, loop the needle under the first stitch to form the final twist in the dove's eye.*

❄ *The Winter Sampler* ❄

Stitch Count: 88 x 162
Design Size: 16.5 x 29.5cm (6½ x 11¾in)
Fabric Selection: Zweigart Cashel linen 28 threads to 2.5cm (1in)
Tapestry Needle Size: 24

This is the last of the four seasonal samplers. It is worked as a band sampler and the stitches needed are described on the chart on pages 175–177 and include cross stitch, back stitch and a number of more unusual counted stitches, pulled thread work and Hardanger embroidery. All the stitches in this sampler are included in the Stitch Library but I recommend that you also read Pulled and Drawn Thread Work and Hardanger Embroidery (pages 66 and 70) before starting to stitch.

The chart is over three pages with no overlapping. You might find it easiest to photocopy the parts and tape them together.

Using stranded cottons (floss) unless otherwise stated, work the cross stitch first, followed by the additional counted stitches and then the Hardanger and other pulled or drawn stitches. Refer to the Stitch Library for the stitch diagrams and relevant instructions as you need them.

Work the Bands as follows:

- Use two strands of stranded cotton for the full and three-quarter cross stitches, eyelet stitches, herringbone, double cross stitch, Algerian eye, French knots, hem stitch, bullion knots and queen stitch.
- Use three strands of stranded cotton for the satin stitch.
- Add back stitch outline where required, using one strand of the colour indicated on the chart
- Work the vertical rice stitch in two colours, the large cross over *four* threads in two strands of stranded cotton and add the small stitches in one strand of gold metallic.
- When working the Algerian eye and double cross stitch, check on the chart whether they are worked over two or four threads.
- For the French knots in the centre of the Christmas roses, work the stitches at random, piling them in groups as shown.
- To form the yellow roses in the top section, work three small French knots in pale green stranded cotton (floss) 368 and then work the bullion bars, filling the needle full to force the stitch to curl slightly.
- Work one row of four-sided stitch around the square as shown on the chart, but work over four threads instead of two.
- For the herringbone, work the top row in 3740 followed by 676 offset by one stitch.
- For the somersault stitch, work two rows of hem stitch following the chart. Working from the centre of the hem-stitched box, carefully snip each horizontal linen thread down the centre line once and using a needle, un-pick the linen threads back to the two outside edges and carefully weave the threads into the fabric thus forming a selvedge. You should be left with vertical threads only.
- Referring to the diagrams on page 113 work one row of somersault stitch as indicated on the chart.

Work the Hardanger as follows:

- Work the Kloster blocks using one strand of perlé cotton No. 5, counting over four threads of the linen. Keep checking that the blocks are directly opposite each other, referring to the diagrams as necessary.
- When all the Kloster blocks are complete, use very sharp, pointed scissors to cut across the ends of the blocks. Take this section slowly, counting and cutting two threads each time.
- Needleweave the remaining linen threads using one strand of perlé cotton No. 8 adding spider's web filling stitch as indicated.
- The diagonal threads included in the two bottom, outer Hardanger motifs are added as the bars are wrapped (as the first stage of the spider's web filling shown on page 121).

Working The Projects

These project instructions are intended for the less experienced stitcher, particularly those who have in the past stitched mainly from kits or perhaps chart packs. The idea of starting a project from scratch is sometimes very daunting so I have included the most useful instructions here so that you can find them at a glance. Refer also to Starting to Stitch on page 16 for further information.

Which Threads Do I Need?

• Each design is charted in the Motif Library with the colour key listing the threads needed to work the project.

Which Fabric and How Much?

• The fabric used, the design size and stitch count of the design is included in the caption under the colour picture.

• If you are working the design exactly as photographed just add a margin of 12.5cm (5in) to the design size and you can move on to 'Where Do I Start'.

• If you wish to use alternative fabrics you must check the thread count of the material and if this is different to that of the stitched sample you must work out the finished design size. To check the thread count of a particular fabric, lay a ruler on top of the material and using a needle

✳ *Winter Gable Cottage* ✳
Stitch Count: 60 x 80
Design Size: 11.5 x 5cm (4½ x 2in)
Fabric Selection: Grey Jobelan 27/28 threads to 2.5cm (1in)
Tapestry Needle Size: 24

This charming design was stitched in two strands of stranded cotton (floss) for the cross stitch and one strand for the back stitch outline. The chart is on page 159 of the Motif Library. See Working the Projects.

count the number of threads or blocks to 2.5cm (1in) and this will tell you the stitch count. (A larger thread count will produce a larger stitched design.) To work out the design size refer to Calculating Design Size on page 17.

Where Do I Start?

• Start stitching in the middle of the design to ensure an adequate margin for stretching and framing.

• To find the middle of the fabric, fold it in four and press lightly. Open out and work a narrow line of tacking (basting) stitches following the threads to mark the fold and the centre. These stitches are removed when the work is completed.

Before You Start

• Rule a line on the chart (if using a copy) to match the tacking (basting) stitches on the fabric.

• Check you have all the colours you need and mount all the threads on a piece of card alongside its shade number (see page 15).

• Sew a narrow hem or oversew the raw edges to prevent fraying. This can be removed on completion. Avoid sticky tape and any clear glues as they have a habit of creeping and will attract grime to your fabric.

• Work one large cross stitch at the top of your work away from the stitching to remind you which is the top and which way the work is facing.

How Many Strands?

• If the chart you wish to stitch does not indicate how many strands of stranded cotton to use, check by carefully pulling a thread from the edge of the fabric and comparing it with the strands of cotton. The threads on the needle should be a similar weight to the threads in the fabric.

• If using alternative threads to the ones used in the stitched sample, try working a few stitches in the fabric margin to check the effect you will achieve.

Finishing Work

• When you have completed the stitching, check the work for missed stitches and press ready for mounting or making up.

Motif Library

I have used a variety of stitched pieces in the book to illustrate a stitching technique or unusual type of thread and you will find the chart within this section of the book.

- The Motif Library charts are illustrated in colour with a black or white symbol added to aid colour identification and to make photo-copying possible.
- Each square, both occupied and unoccupied, represents two threads of evenweave or one block of Aida unless stated otherwise.
- Each occupied square on a chart equals one stitch.
- A three-quarter cross stitch is shown as a triangle occupying half a square.
- All that determines the size of a cross stitch

design is the number stitches up and down and the choice of fabric.

- All of the designs in the Motif Library may be worked in cross stitch but you may like to experiment using other stitches.
- DMC stranded cottons were used but alternatives are given where appropriate, such as Anchor stranded cotton or Beadesign.
- Some of the designs are charted over two pages: there is no overlap, just continue stitching. You could photocopy the two parts of the charts and stick them together.
- Back stitches are shown by an arrow pointing to a solid line, with the DMC colour beside it.
- The four small arrows on each chart will help you find the centre quikly.

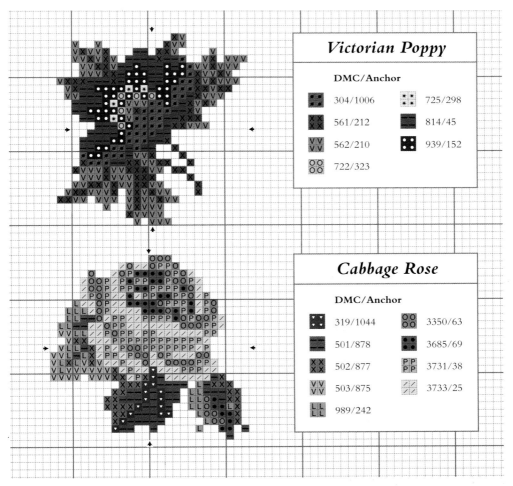

Victorian Poppy

DMC/Anchor

304/1006		725/298	
561/212		814/45	
562/210		939/152	
722/323			

Cabbage Rose

DMC/Anchor

319/1044		3350/63	
501/878		3685/69	
502/877		3731/38	
503/875		3733/25	
989/242			

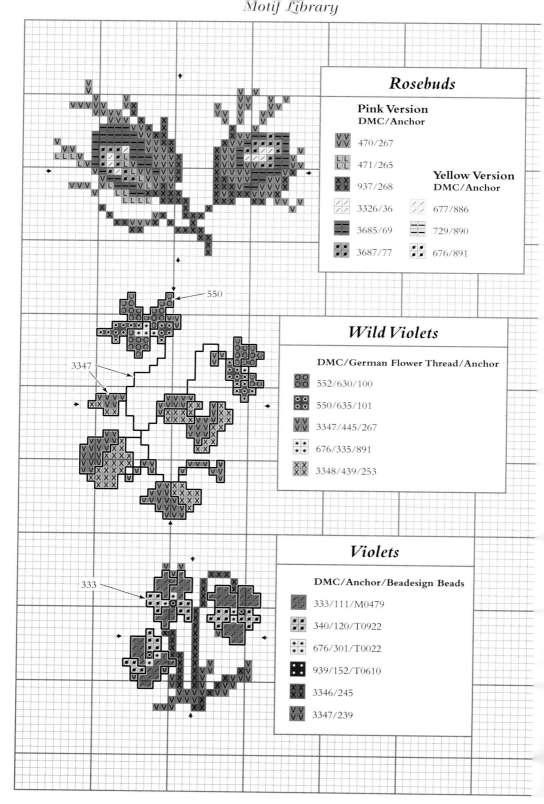

Rosebuds

Pink Version
DMC/Anchor

V V / V V	470/267
L L / L L	471/265
X X	937/268
3326/36	
3685/69	
3687/77	

Yellow Version
DMC/Anchor

677/886	
729/890	
676/891	

Wild Violets

DMC/German Flower Thread/Anchor

O O / O O	552/630/100
O O / O O	550/635/101
V V / V V	3347/445/267
* * / * *	676/335/891
X X / X X	3348/439/253

550

3347

Violets

DMC/Anchor/Beadesign Beads

333/111/M0479	
340/120/T0922	
* * / * *	676/301/T0022
939/152/T0610	
X X / X X	3346/245
V V / V V	3347/239

333

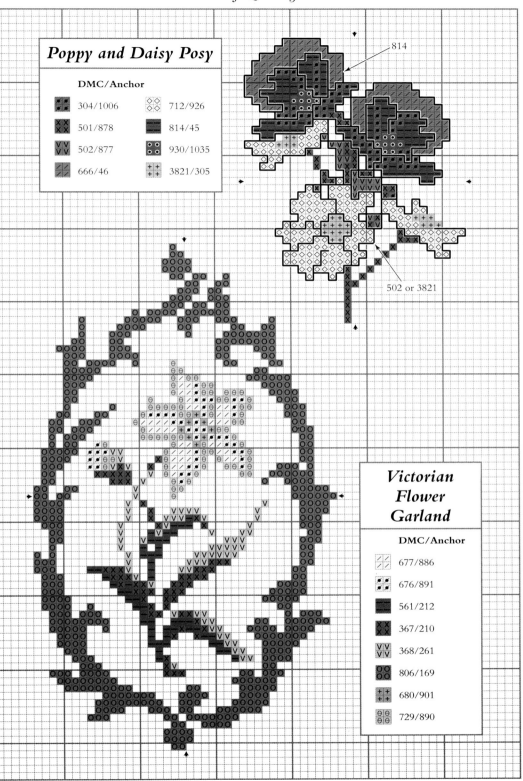

Poppy and Daisy Posy

DMC/Anchor

304/1006		712/926
501/878		814/45
502/877		930/1035
666/46		3821/305

814

502 or 3821

Victorian Flower Garland

DMC/Anchor

677/886
676/891
561/212
367/210
368/261
806/169
680/901
729/890

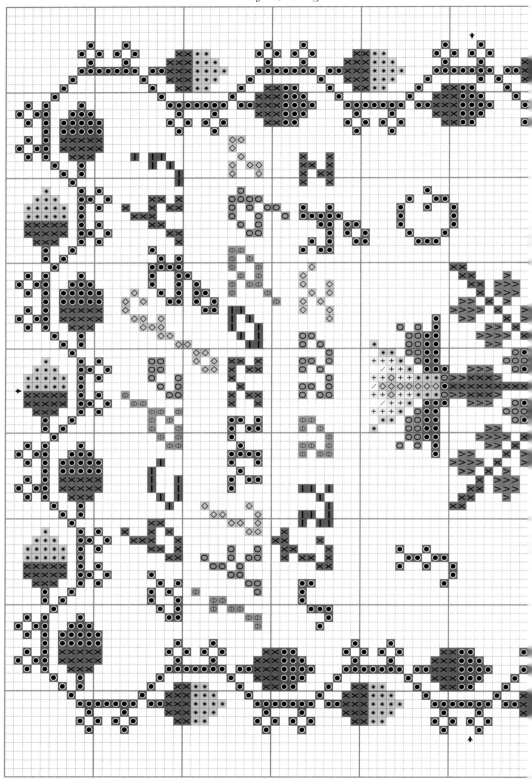

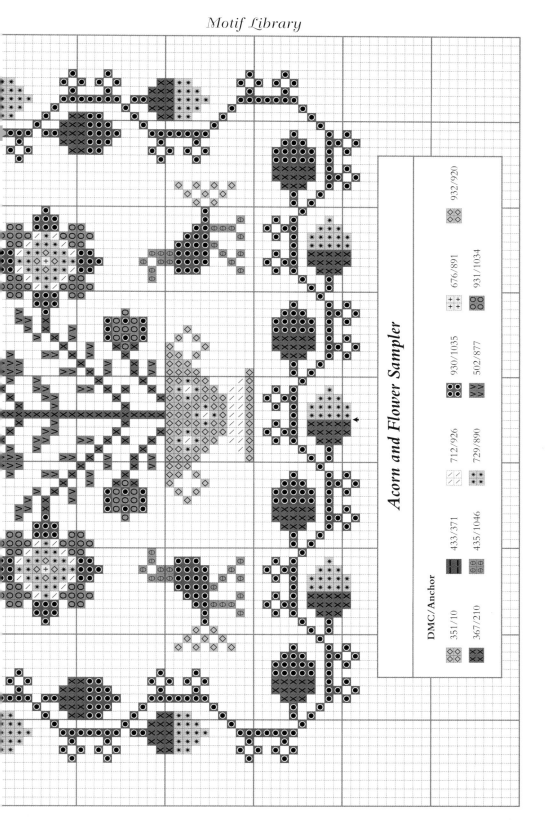

Acorn and Flower Sampler

DMC/Anchor

351/10	433/371	712/926	930/1035
367/210	435/1046	729/890	502/877
		676/891	932/920
		931/1034	

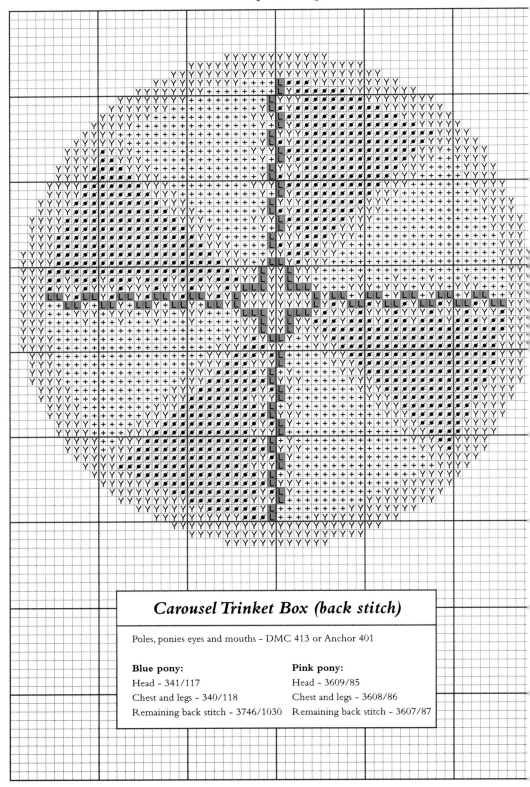

Carousel Trinket Box (back stitch)

Poles, ponies eyes and mouths – DMC 413 or Anchor 401

Blue pony:
Head – 341/117
Chest and legs – 340/118
Remaining back stitch – 3746/1030

Pink pony:
Head – 3609/85
Chest and legs – 3608/86
Remaining back stitch – 3607/87

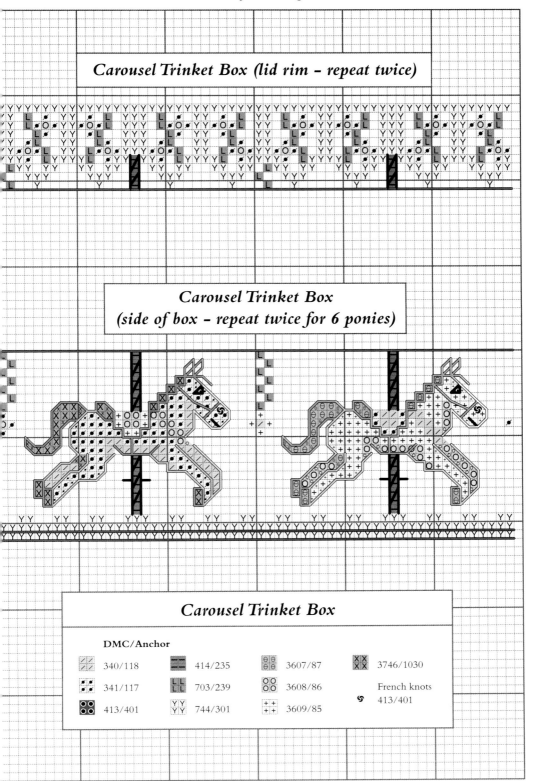

Carousel Trinket Box (lid rim – repeat twice)

Carousel Trinket Box
(side of box – repeat twice for 6 ponies)

Carousel Trinket Box

DMC/Anchor

340/118	414/235	3607/87	3746/1030
341/117	703/239	3608/86	French knots
413/401	744/301	3609/85	413/401

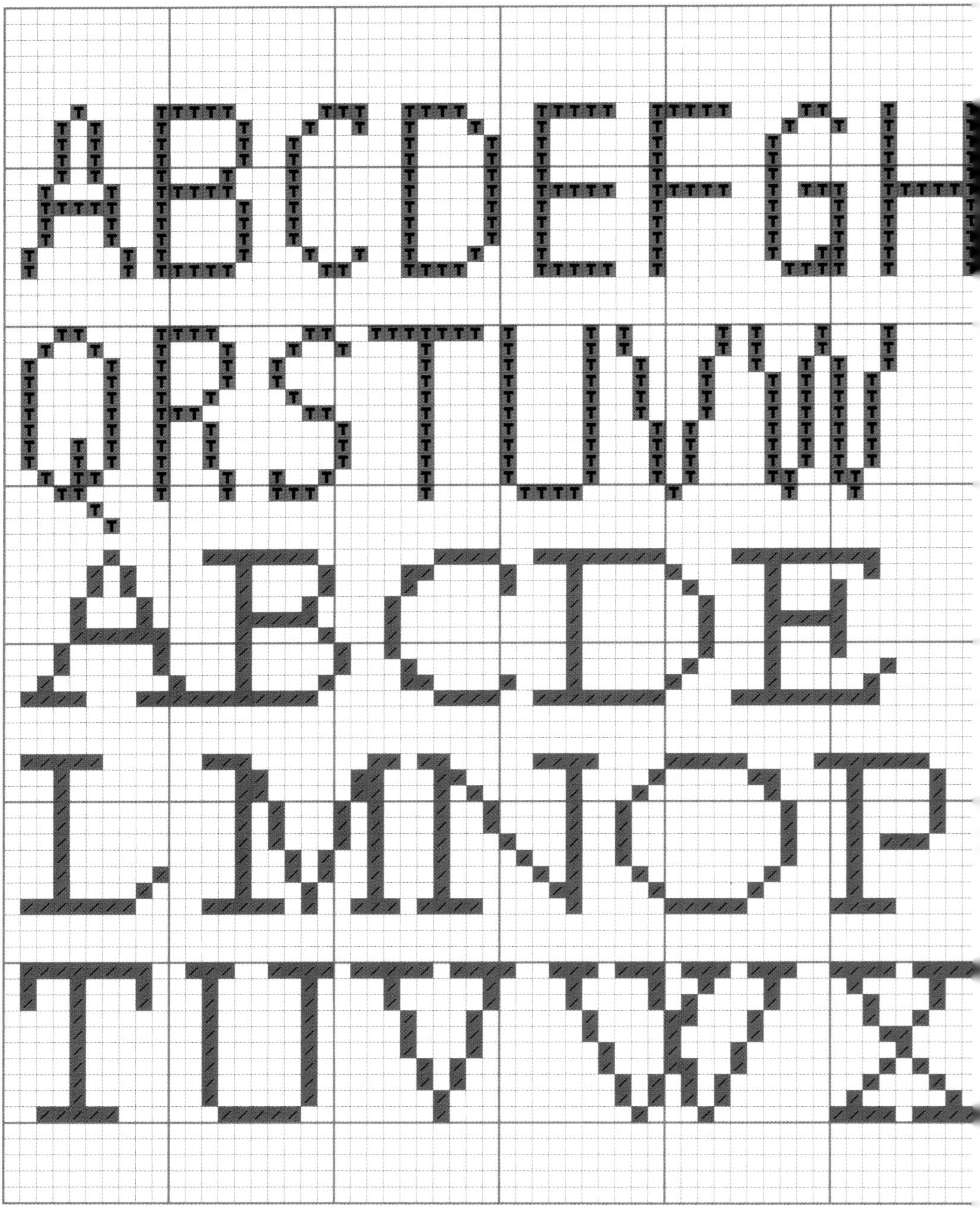
ABCDEFGH
QRSTUVW
ABCDE
LMNOP
TUVWX

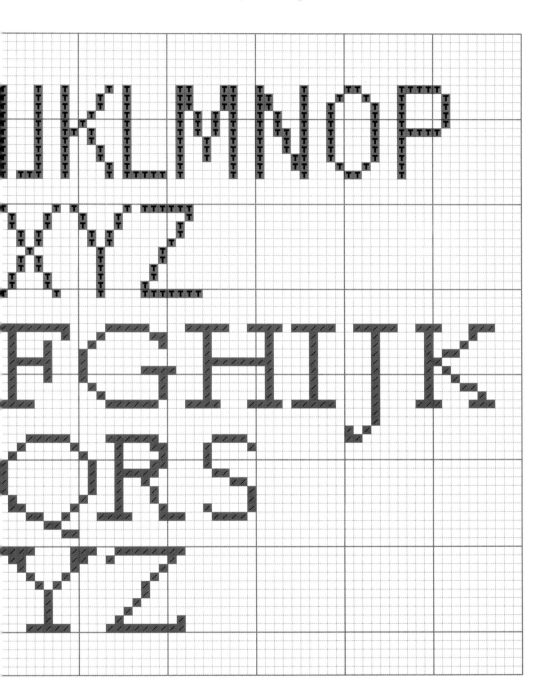

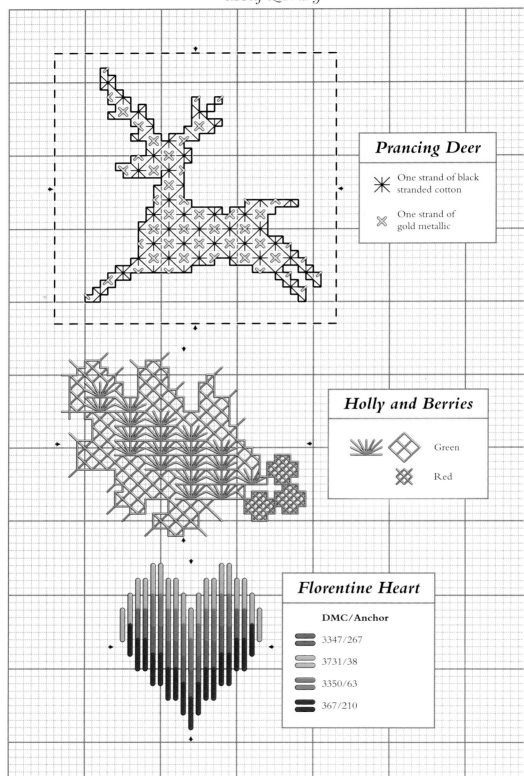

Prancing Deer

※ One strand of black stranded cotton

✕ One strand of gold metallic

Holly and Berries

◇ Green

✕ Red

Florentine Heart

DMC/Anchor

3347/267

3731/38

3350/63

367/210

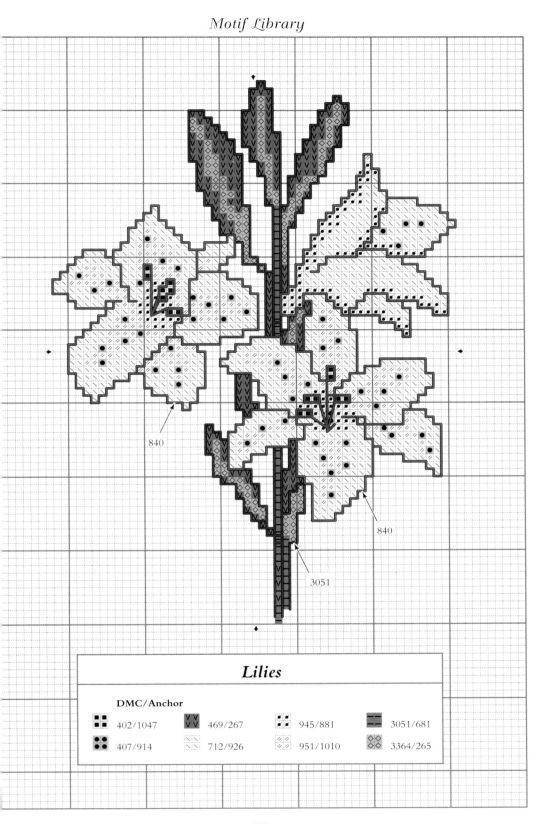

840

840

3051

Lilies

DMC/Anchor

▪▪ 402/1047	⊽⊽ 469/267	⦂⦂ 945/881	▬▬ 3051/681
●● 407/914	⟍⟍ 712/926	⁄⁄ 951/1010	◇◇ 3364/265

Cat on a Wall

DMC/Anchor

310/403
712/926
367/210
368/261
437/1045
435/1046
436/901
3364/265

310

436

Berlin Rose Posy

DMC/Anchor

	223/895	LL	470/267
	224/894	++	471/265
	225/1026		472/253
	319/1044		818/48
V V	320/215		3685/69
X X	367/210		

Bells

DMC/Anchor

	304/1006
	666/46
Y Y	676/891
	729/890
X X	909/923
V V	911/205
**	metallic gold

304

729

304

Poinsettia

DMC/Anchor

	304/1006		909/923	++	912/204
	666/46	V V	911/205		French knot 725/298

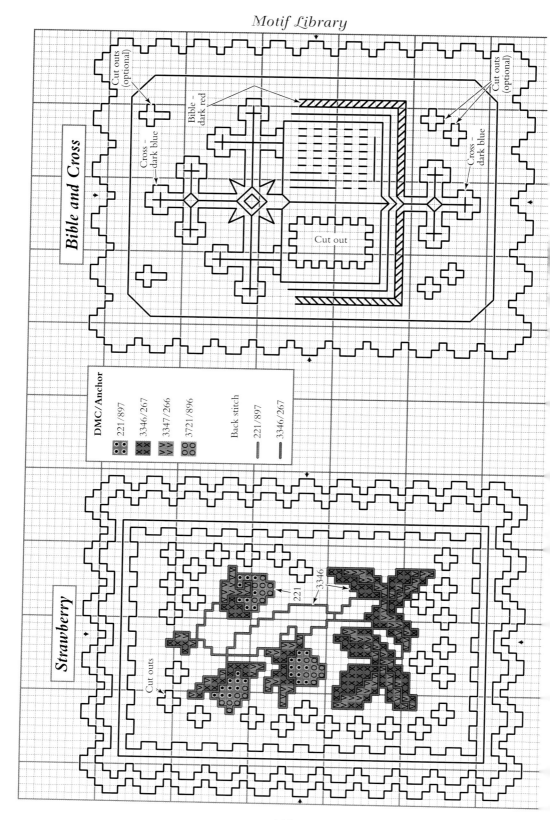

Bible and Cross

Cut outs (optional)

Bible – dark red

Cross – dark blue

Cut outs (optional)

Cross – dark blue

Cut out

DMC/Anchor

○○ ○○	221/897
✗✗ ✗✗	3346/267
V V V V	3347/266
○○ ○○	3721/896

Back stitch

——— 221/897

——— 3346/267

Strawberry

Cut outs

221

3346

3346

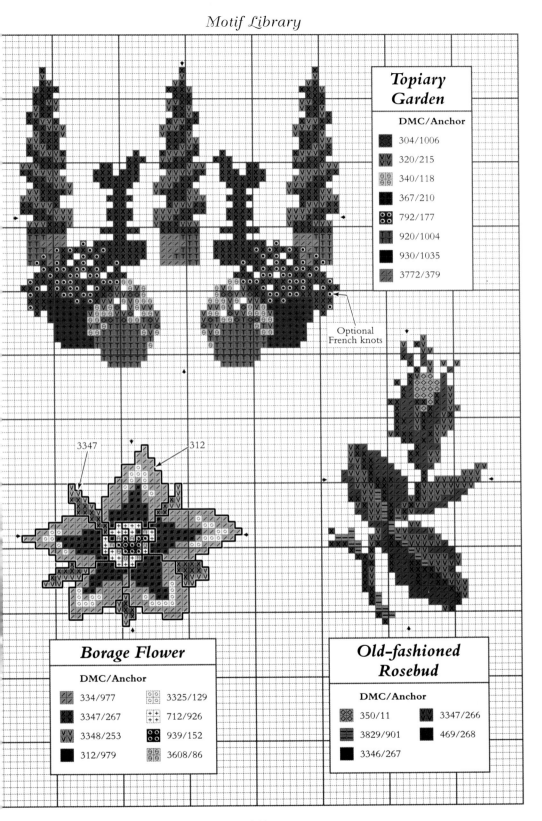

Topiary Garden

DMC/Anchor

- 304/1006
- 320/215
- 340/118
- 367/210
- 792/177
- 920/1004
- 930/1035
- 3772/379

Optional French knots

3347   312

Borage Flower

DMC/Anchor

334/977		3325/129
3347/267		712/926
3348/253		939/152
312/979		3608/86

Old-fashioned Rosebud

DMC/Anchor

350/11		3347/266
3829/901		469/268
3346/267		

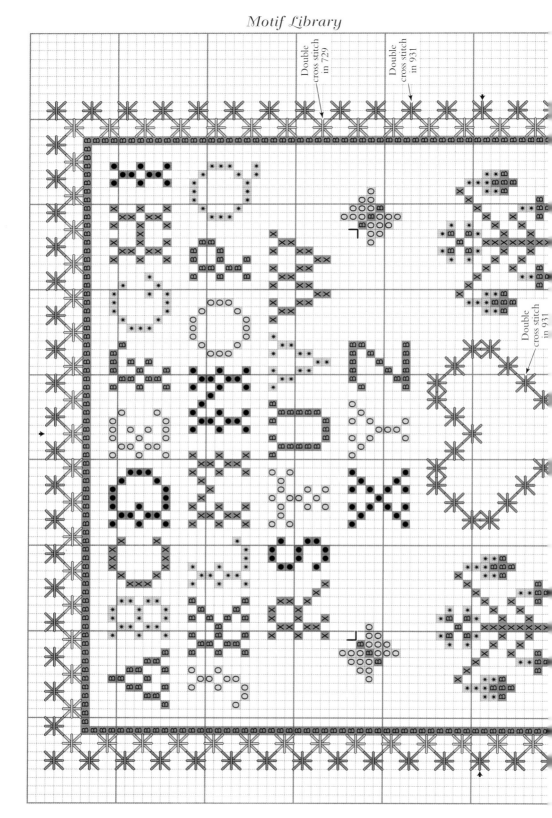

Double cross stitch in 729

Double cross stitch in 931

Double cross stitch in 931

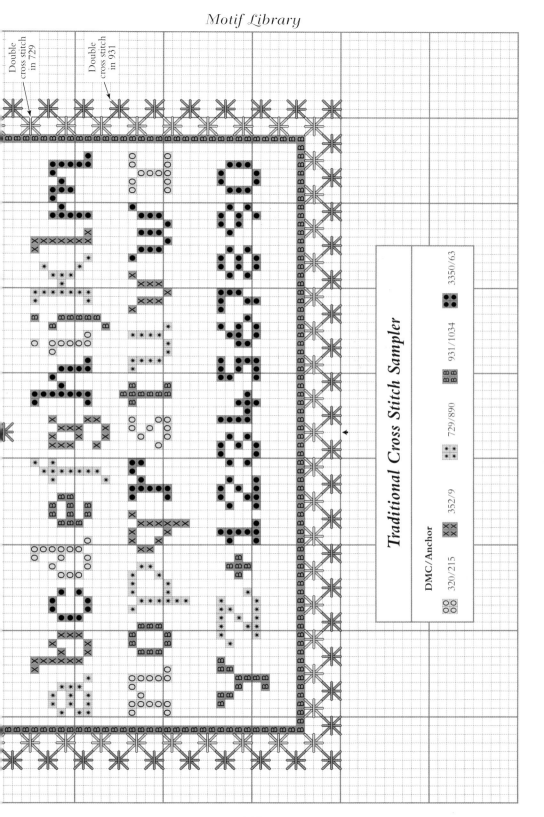

Double cross stitch in 729

Double cross stitch in 931

Traditional Cross Stitch Sampler

DMC/Anchor

320/215 352/9 729/890 931/1034 3350/63

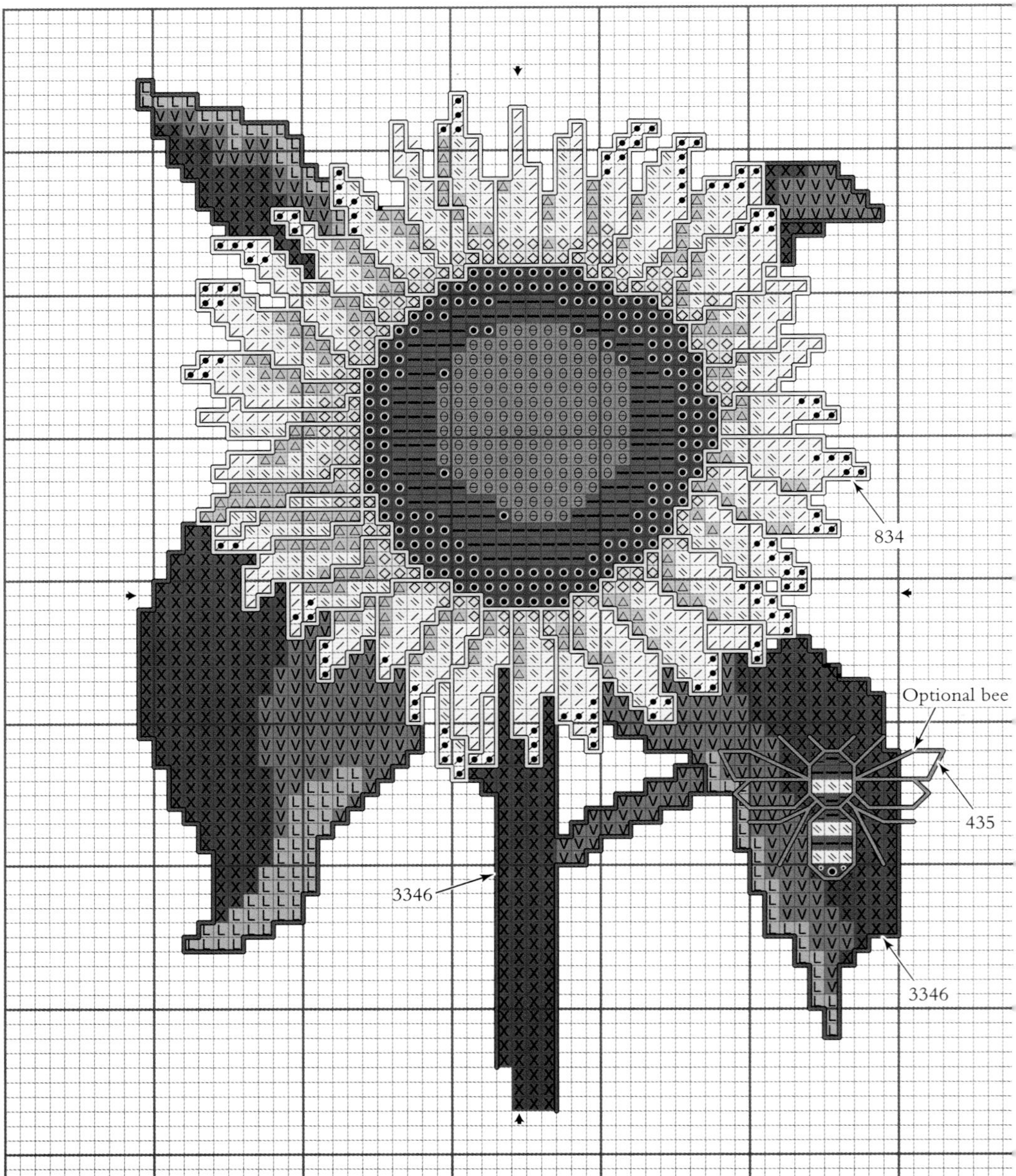

834

Optional bee

435

3346

3346

Sunflower

DMC Stranded Cotton/Appleton Crewel Wool

433/957	676/472	834/477	3348/332
434/911	725/471	3346/346	3821/844
435/903	744/695	3347/345	

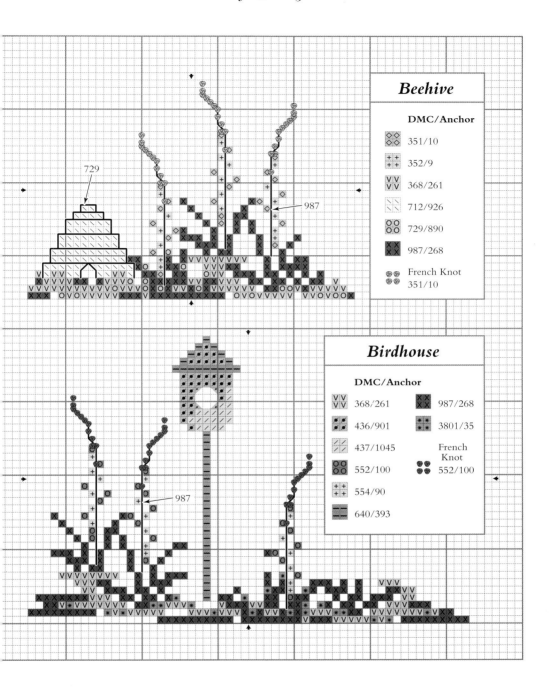

Beehive

DMC/Anchor

◇◇	351/10
++	352/9
VV	368/261
\\	712/926
OO	729/890
XX	987/268
🌀🌀	French Knot 351/10

729

987

Birdhouse

DMC/Anchor

VV	368/261	XX	987/268
✹✹	436/901	✱✱	3801/35
⁄⁄	437/1045		French Knot
OO	552/100	●●	552/100
++	554/90		
▬▬	640/393		

987

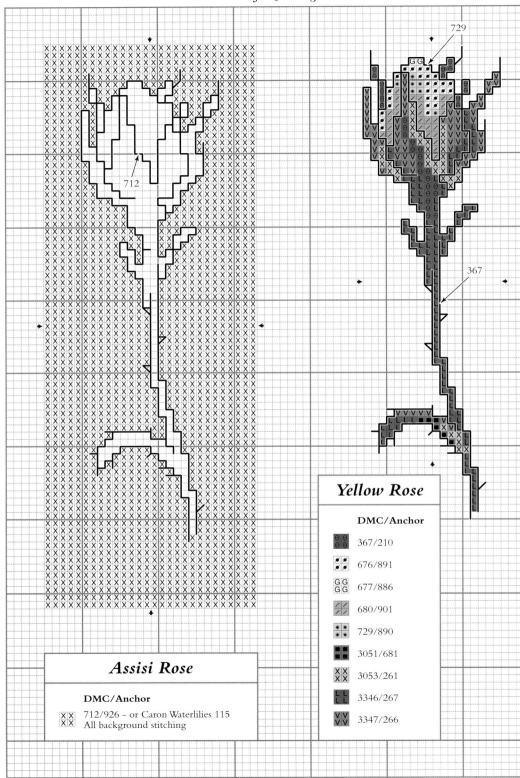

712

729

367

Yellow Rose

DMC/Anchor

367/210
676/891
677/886
680/901
729/890
3051/681
3053/261
3346/267
3347/266

Assisi Rose

DMC/Anchor

X X 712/926 – or Caron Waterlilies 115
X X All background stitching

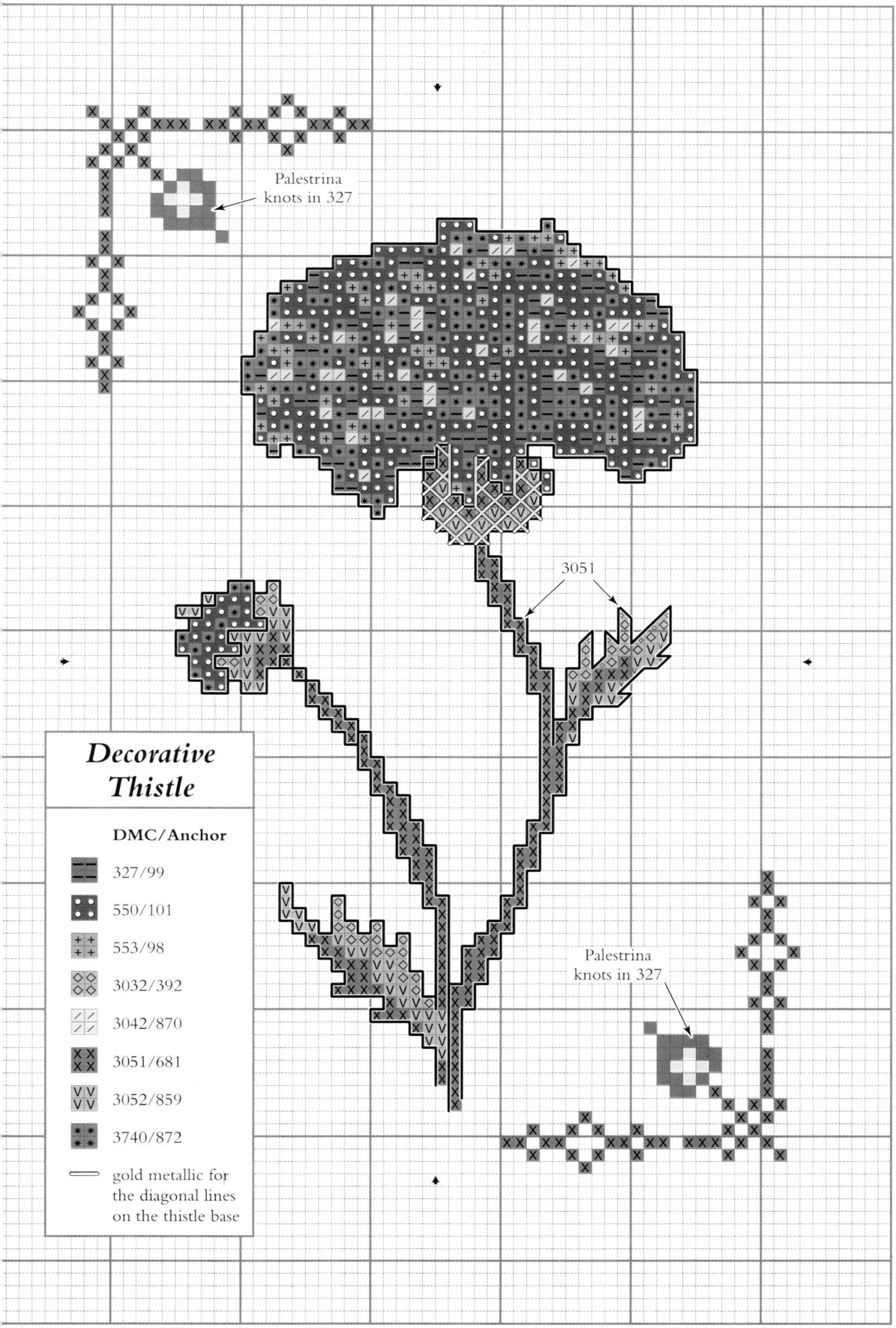

Palestrina
knots in 327

3051

Decorative Thistle

DMC/Anchor

▓	327/99
⦂⦂	550/101
+ + / + +	553/98
◇◇	3032/392
⁄⁄ / ⁄⁄	3042/870
XX / XX	3051/681
V V / V V	3052/859
∗∗ / ∗∗	3740/872
──	gold metallic for the diagonal lines on the thistle base

Palestrina
knots in 327

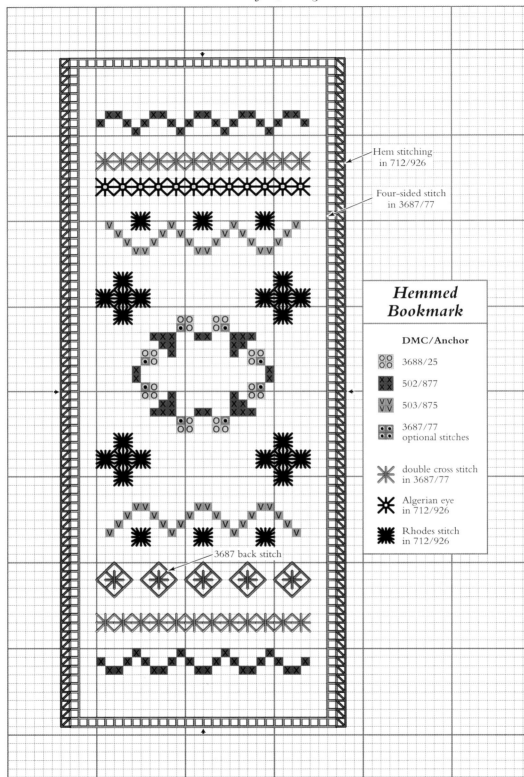

Hem stitching
in 712/926

Four-sided stitch
in 3687/77

3687 back stitch

Hemmed Bookmark

DMC/Anchor

3688/25

502/877

503/875

3687/77
optional stitches

double cross stitch
in 3687/77

Algerian eye
in 712/926

Rhodes stitch
in 712/926

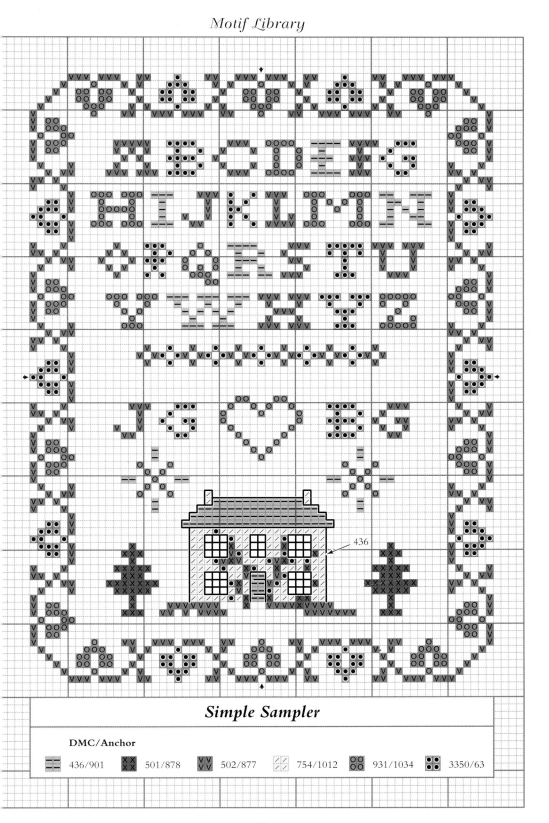

Simple Sampler

DMC/Anchor

436/901	501/878	502/877	754/1012	931/1034	3350/63

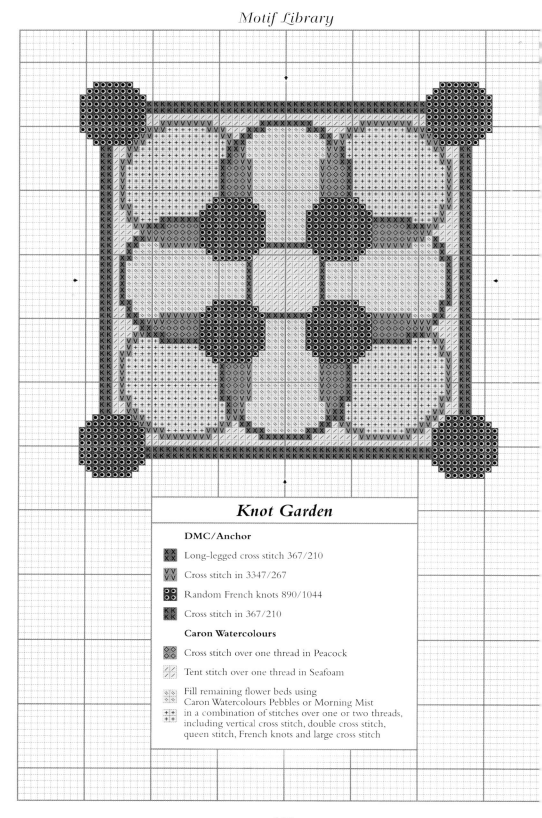

Knot Garden

DMC/Anchor

Long-legged cross stitch 367/210

Cross stitch in 3347/267

Random French knots 890/1044

Cross stitch in 367/210

Caron Watercolours

Cross stitch over one thread in Peacock

Tent stitch over one thread in Seafoam

Fill remaining flower beds using
Caron Watercolours Pebbles or Morning Mist
in a combination of stitches over one or two threads,
including vertical cross stitch, double cross stitch,
queen stitch, French knots and large cross stitch

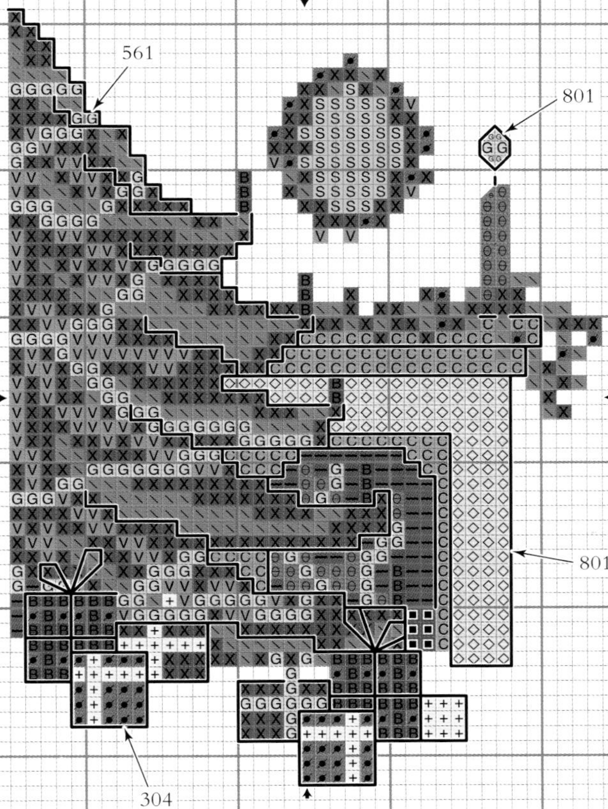

Christmas Tree

DMC/Anchor

▪▪	304/1006
▦	310/403
XX	561/212
VV	562/210
++	676/891
▬	801/359
BB	797/132
▨	5269
▨	5270
CC	5279 } no exchange
GG	5282
SS	5283
◇◇	Marlitt Cream Rayon

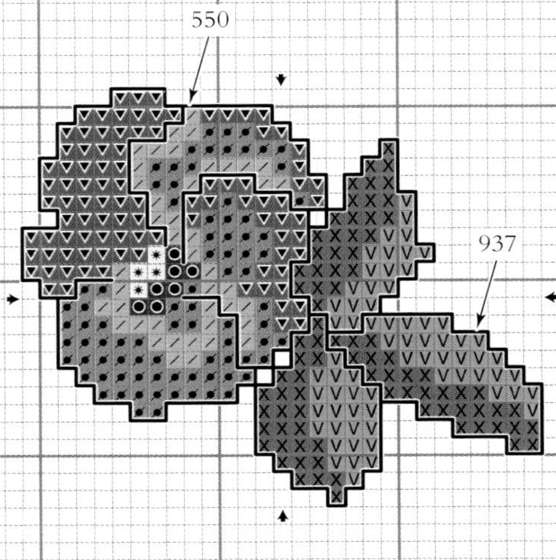

Purple Pansy

DMC/Anchor

VV	470/267
▼▼	550/101
▪▪	552/100
◿	553/98
✱✱	676/891
XX	937/268
◐◐	939/152

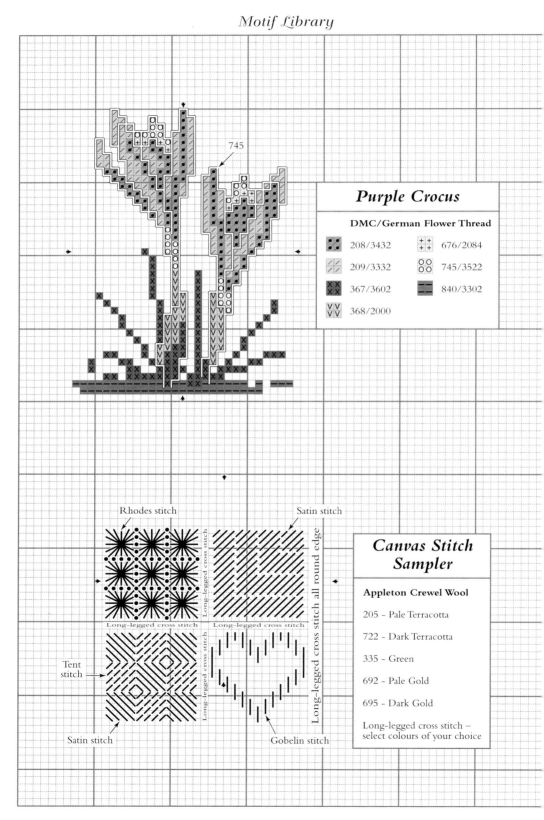

745

Purple Crocus

DMC/German Flower Thread

●● ●●	208/3432	+ + + +	676/2084
⁄⁄ ⁄⁄	209/3332	○○ ○○	745/3522
✗✗ ✗✗	367/3602	▬▬	840/3302
ⱽⱽ ⱽⱽ	368/2000		

Rhodes stitch

Satin stitch

Long-legged cross stitch

Long-legged cross stitch all round edge

Canvas Stitch Sampler

Appleton Crewel Wool

205 – Pale Terracotta

722 – Dark Terracotta

335 – Green

692 – Pale Gold

695 – Dark Gold

Long-legged cross stitch – select colours of your choice

Long-legged cross stitch

Long-legged cross stitch

Tent stitch

Satin stitch

Gobelin stitch

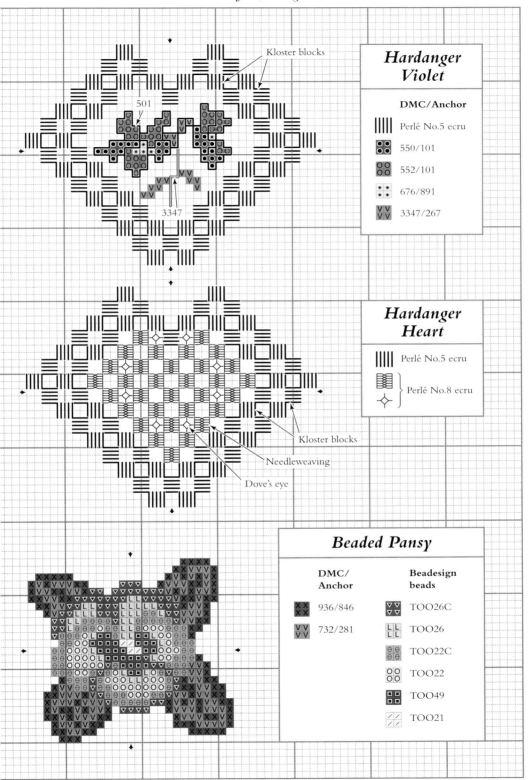

Kloster blocks

Hardanger Violet

DMC/Anchor

IIII	Perlé No.5 ecru
550/101
552/101
676/891
3347/267

501

3347

Hardanger Heart

IIII	Perlé No.5 ecru
} Perlé No.8 ecru

Kloster blocks

Needleweaving

Dove's eye

Beaded Pansy

DMC/ Anchor		Beadesign beads
936/846		TOO26C
732/281		TOO26
		TOO22C
		TOO22
		TOO49
		TOO21

840

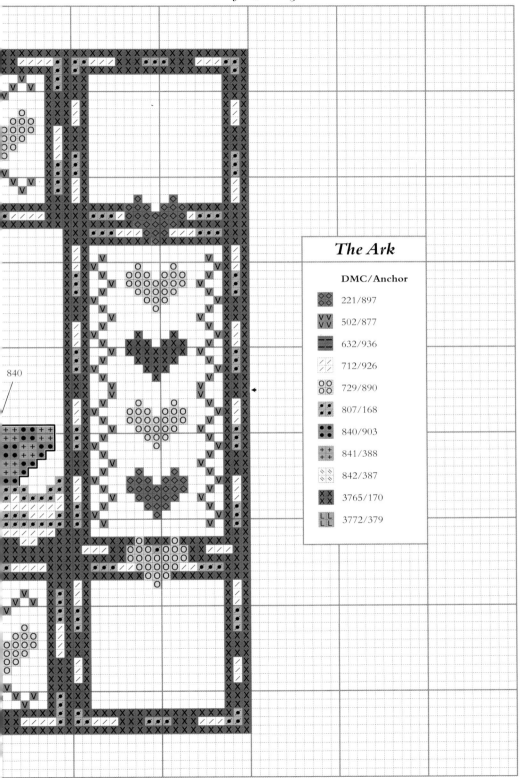

840

The Ark

DMC/Anchor

221/897
502/877
632/936
712/926
729/890
807/168
840/903
841/388
842/387
3765/170
3772/379

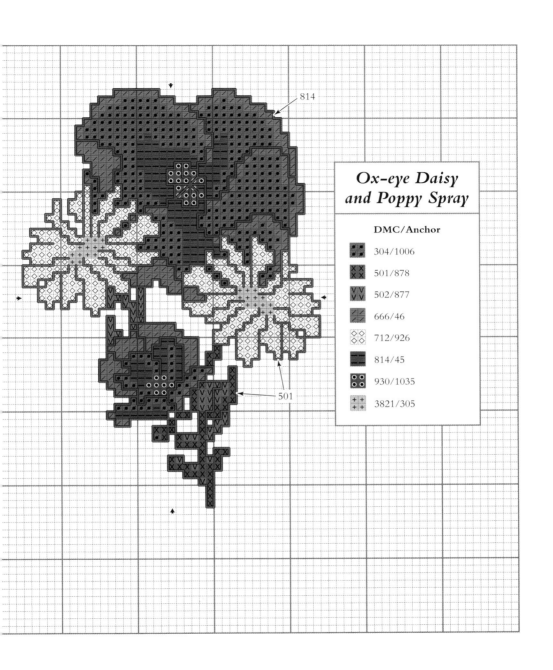

814

**Ox-eye Daisy
and Poppy Spray**

DMC/Anchor

304/1006
501/878
502/877
666/46
712/926
814/45
930/1035
3821/305

501

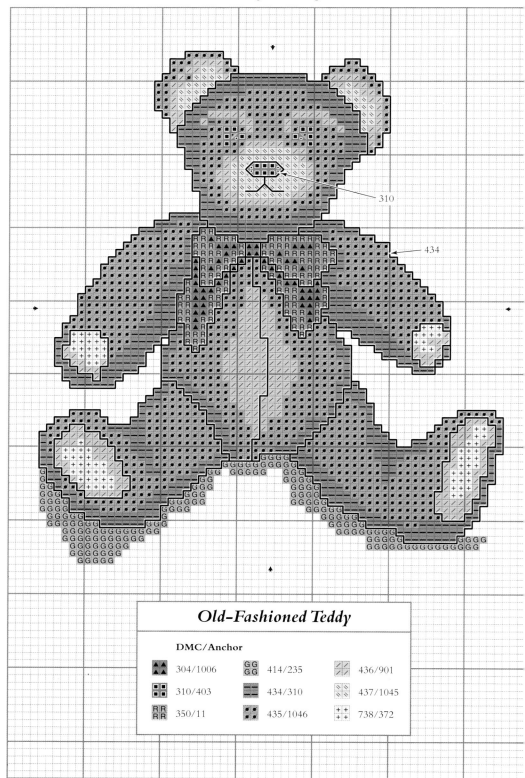

310

434

Old-Fashioned Teddy

DMC/Anchor

▲▲	304/1006	GG	414/235	⁄⁄	436/901
■■	310/403	▬	434/310	⁍⁍	437/1045
RR	350/11	▪▪	435/1046	++	738/372

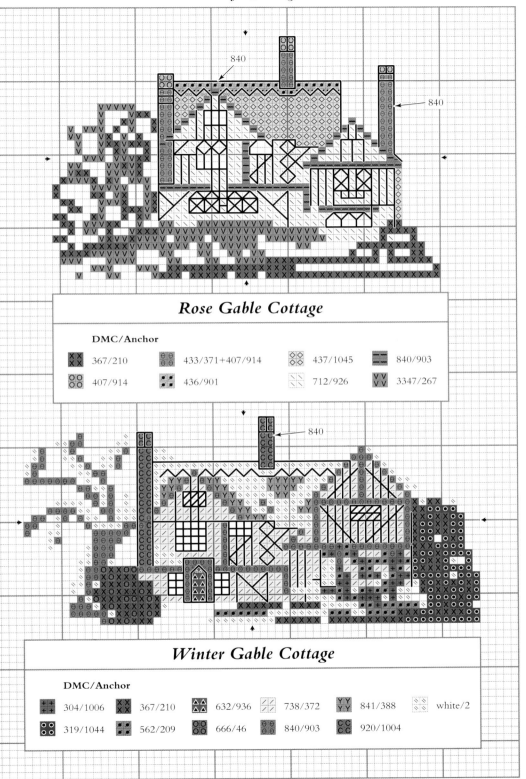

Rose Gable Cottage

DMC/Anchor

XX 367/210	433/371+407/914	437/1045	840/903
OO 407/914	436/901	712/926	VV 3347/267

Winter Gable Cottage

DMC/Anchor

++ 304/1006	XX 367/210	AA 632/936	738/372	YY 841/388	white/2
319/1044	562/209	OO 666/46	840/903	CC 920/1004	

841

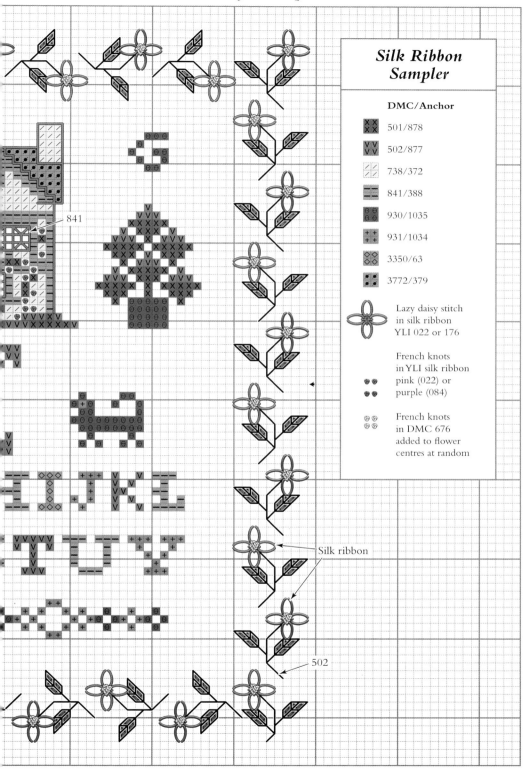

Silk Ribbon Sampler

DMC/Anchor

XX	501/878
VV	502/877
	738/372
	841/388
	930/1035
++	931/1034
	3350/63
	3772/379

Lazy daisy stitch in silk ribbon YLI 022 or 176

French knots in YLI silk ribbon pink (022) or purple (084)

French knots in DMC 676 added to flower centres at random

841

Silk ribbon

502

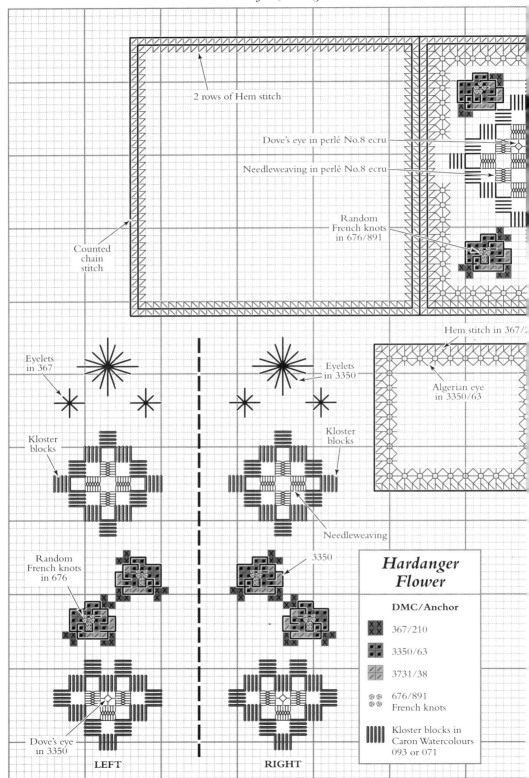

2 rows of Hem stitch

Dove's eye in perlé No.8 ecru

Needleweaving in perlé No.8 ecru

Random
French knots
in 676/891

Counted
chain
stitch

Hem stitch in 367/2

Algerian eye
in 3350/63

Eyelets
in 367

Eyelets
in 3350

Kloster
blocks

Kloster
blocks

Needleweaving

Random
French knots
in 676

3350

Dove's eye
in 3350

LEFT

RIGHT

Hardanger Flower

DMC/Anchor

❎❎	367/210
▦	3350/63
▨	3731/38
🌼🌼	676/891 French knots
▥▥▥	Kloster blocks in Caron Watercolours 093 or 071

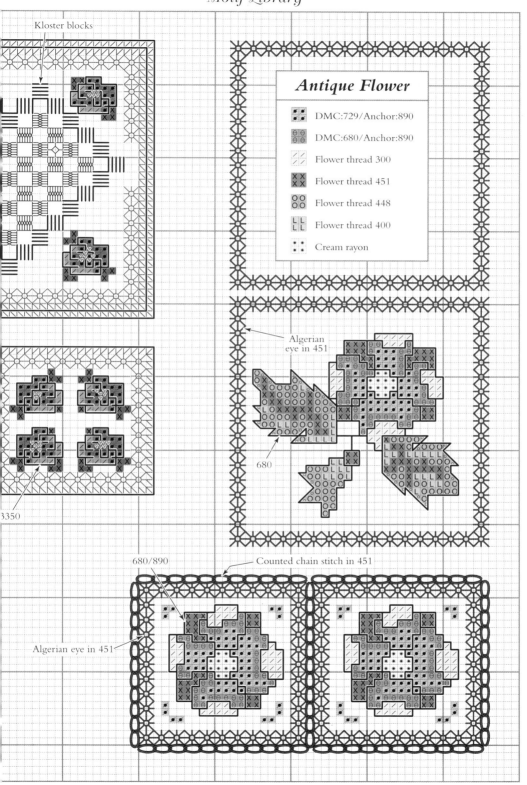

Kloster blocks

Antique Flower

● ●	DMC:729/Anchor:890
⊖ ⊖	DMC:680/Anchor:890
∕ ∕	Flower thread 300
X X	Flower thread 451
O O	Flower thread 448
L L	Flower thread 400
∗ ∗	Cream rayon

Algerian eye in 451

680

3350

680/890 — Counted chain stitch in 451

Algerian eye in 451

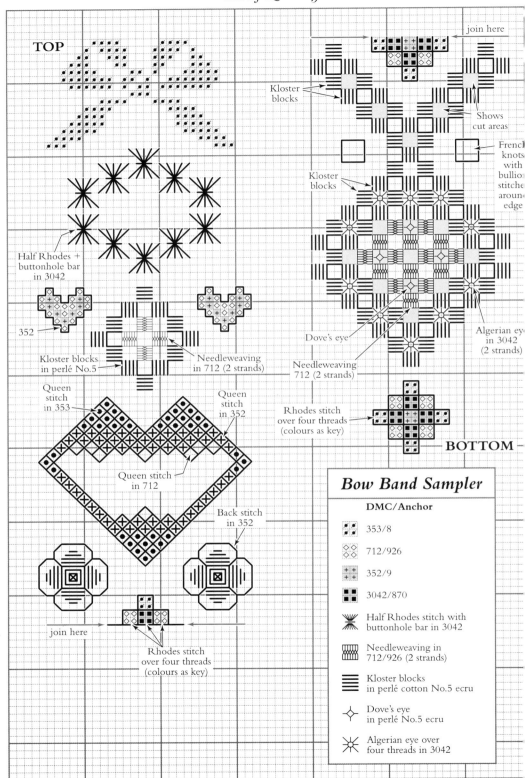

TOP

join here

Kloster blocks

Shows cut areas

French knots with bullion stitches around edge

Kloster blocks

Half Rhodes + buttonhole bar in 3042

352

Kloster blocks in perlé No.5

Needleweaving in 712 (2 strands)

Dove's eye

Algerian eye in 3042 (2 strands)

Needleweaving 712 (2 strands)

Queen stitch in 353

Queen stitch in 352

Rhodes stitch over four threads (colours as key)

Queen stitch in 712

BOTTOM

Back stitch in 352

join here

Rhodes stitch over four threads (colours as key)

Bow Band Sampler

DMC/Anchor

353/8	
712/926	
352/9	
3042/870	

Half Rhodes stitch with buttonhole bar in 3042

Needleweaving in 712/926 (2 strands)

Kloster blocks in perlé cotton No.5 ecru

Dove's eye in perlé No.5 ecru

Algerian eye over four threads in 3042

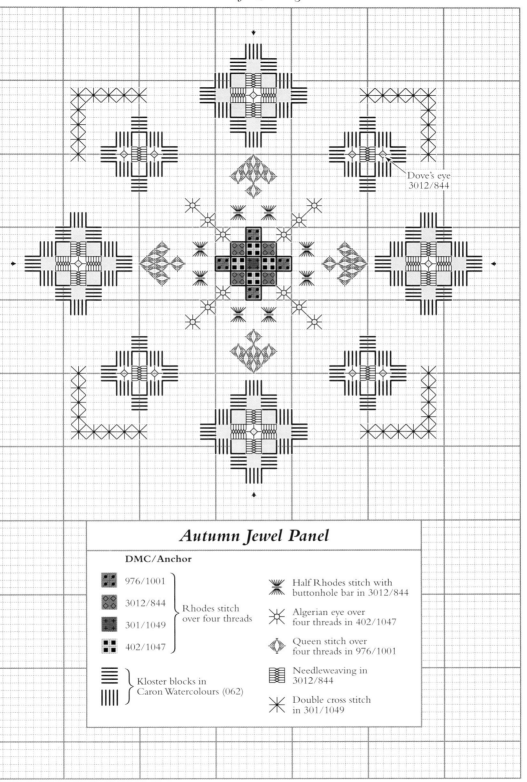

Dove's eye
3012/844

Autumn Jewel Panel

DMC/Anchor

976/1001
3012/844 } Rhodes stitch
over four threads
301/1049
402/1047

≡ } Kloster blocks in
‖‖ Caron Watercolours (062)

Half Rhodes stitch with
buttonhole bar in 3012/844

Algerian eye over
four threads in 402/1047

Queen stitch over
four threads in 976/1001

Needleweaving in
3012/844

Double cross stitch
in 301/1049

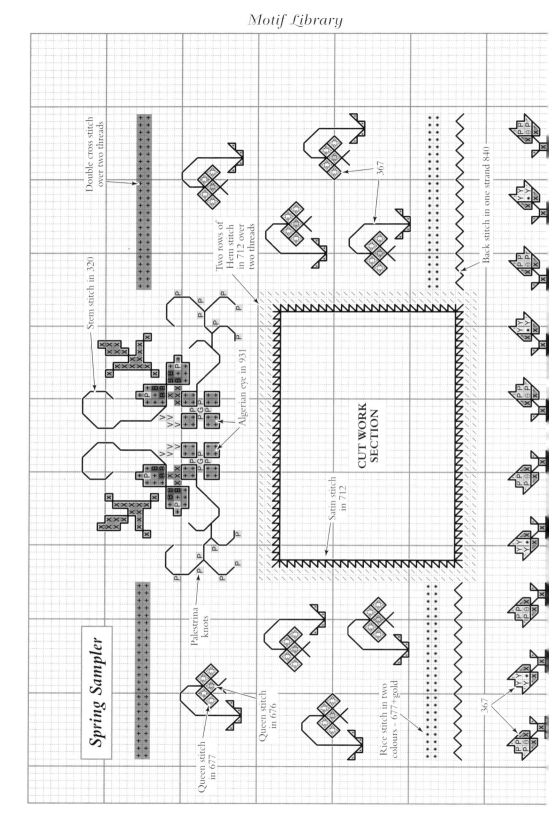

Spring Sampler

Double cross stitch over two threads

Stem stitch in 320

Two rows of Hem stitch in 712 over two threads

367

Back stitch in one strand 840

Algerian eye in 931

Palestrina knots

Satin stitch in 712

CUT WORK SECTION

Queen stitch in 677

Queen stitch in 676

Rice stitch in two colours – 677+gold

367

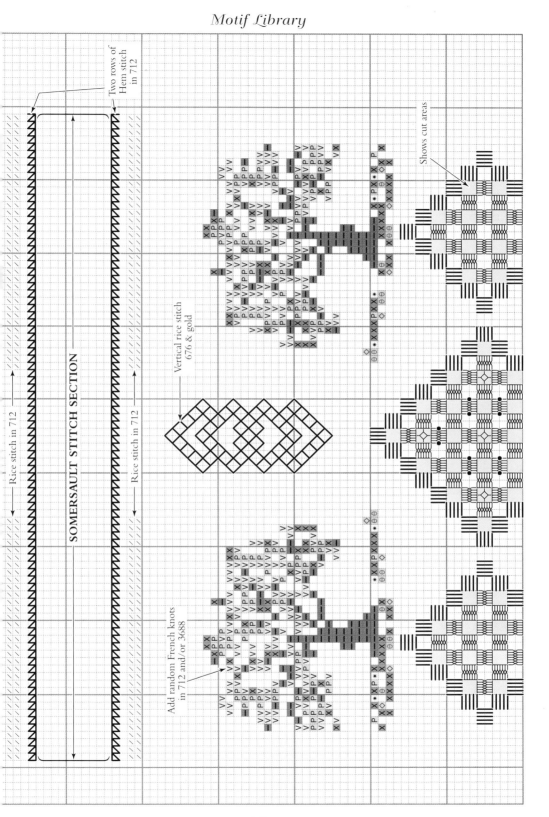

Two rows of Hem stitch in 712

Shows cut areas

Rice stitch in 712

SOMERSAULT STITCH SECTION

Rice stitch in 712

Vertical rice stitch 676 & gold

Add random French knots in 712 and/or 3688

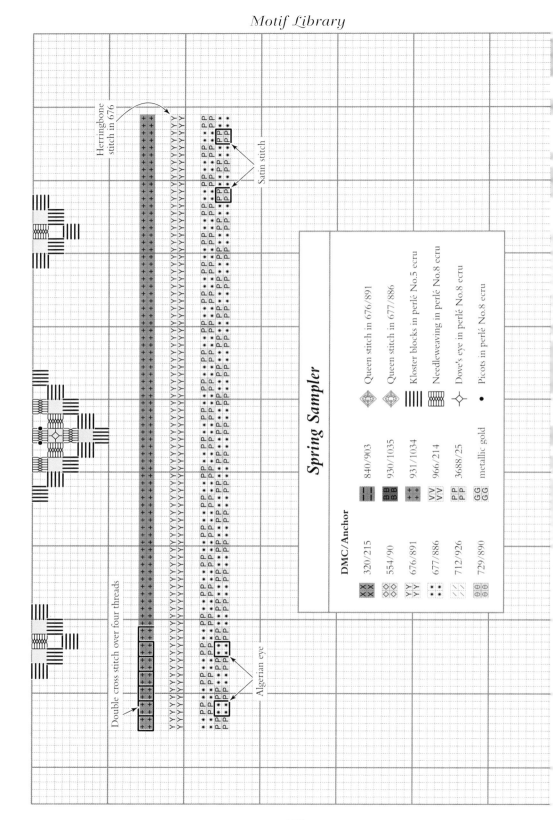

Herringbone stitch in 676

Satin stitch

Double cross stitch over four threads

Algerian eye

Spring Sampler

◈ Queen stitch in 676/891

◈ Queen stitch in 677/886

||| Kloster blocks in perlé No.5 ecru

▦ Needleweaving in perlé No.8 ecru

◇ Dove's eye in perlé No.8 ecru

• Picots in perlé No.8 ecru

DMC/Anchor

XX	320/215	
◇◇	554/90	
YY	676/891	
**	677/886	
╲╲	712/926	
ΘΘ	729/890	
▌▌	840/903	
BB	930/1035	
++	931/1034	
VV	966/214	
PP	3688/25	
GG	metallic gold	

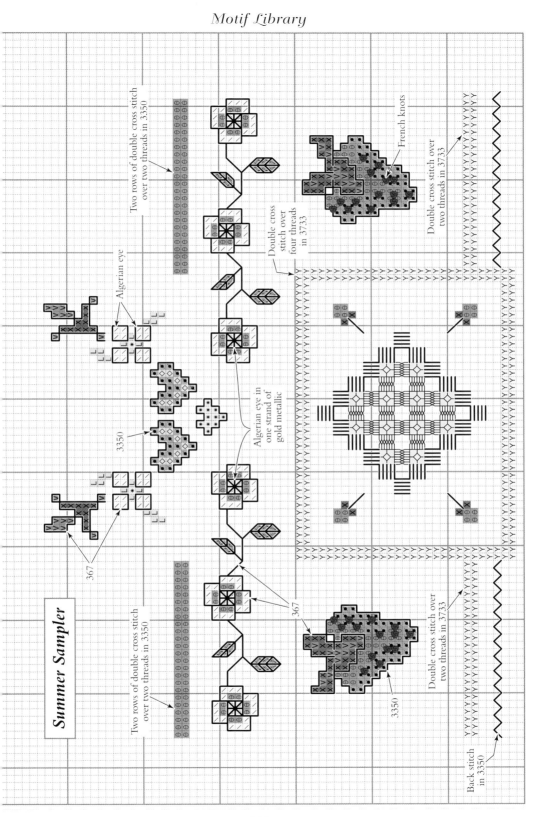

Summer Sampler

Two rows of double cross stitch over two threads in 3350

French knots

Double cross stitch over two threads in 3733

Double cross stitch over four threads in 3733

Algerian eye

367

3350

Algerian eye in one strand of gold metallic

367

Two rows of double cross stitch over two threads in 3350

3350

Double cross stitch over two threads in 3733

Back stitch in 3350

Queen stitch

367

Algerian eye over four threads in 712

367

Queen stitch in shades as shown

Algerian eye over four threads in 712

3685

Algerian eye

3685

Queen stitch

367

Rhodes stitch

shows cut areas

Rhodes stitch

Rhodes stitch

Back stitch outline in 3685

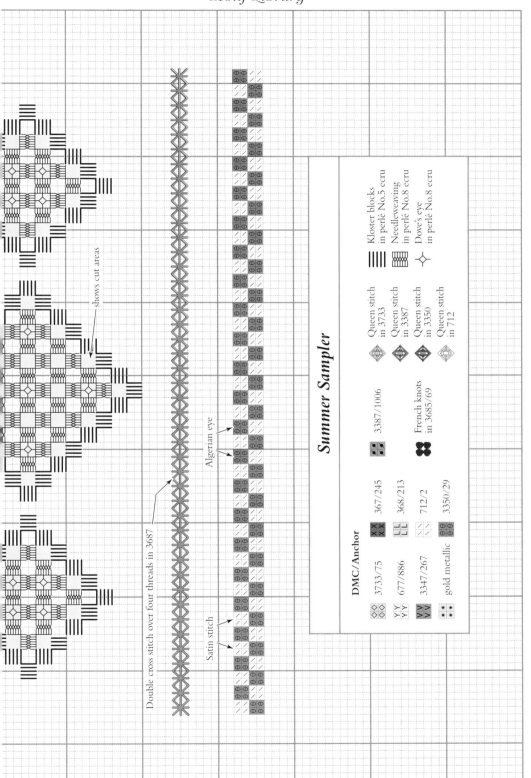

shows cut areas

Double cross stitch over four threads in 3687

Algerian eye

Satin stitch

Summer Sampler

DMC/Anchor

3733/75	367/245	3387/1006	Queen stitch in 3733
677/886	368/213		Queen stitch in 3387
3347/267	712/2	French knots in 3685/69	Queen stitch in 3350
gold metallic	3350/29		Queen stitch in 712

Kloster blocks in perlé No.5 ecru

Needleweaving in perlé No.8 ecru

Dove's eye in perlé No.8 ecru

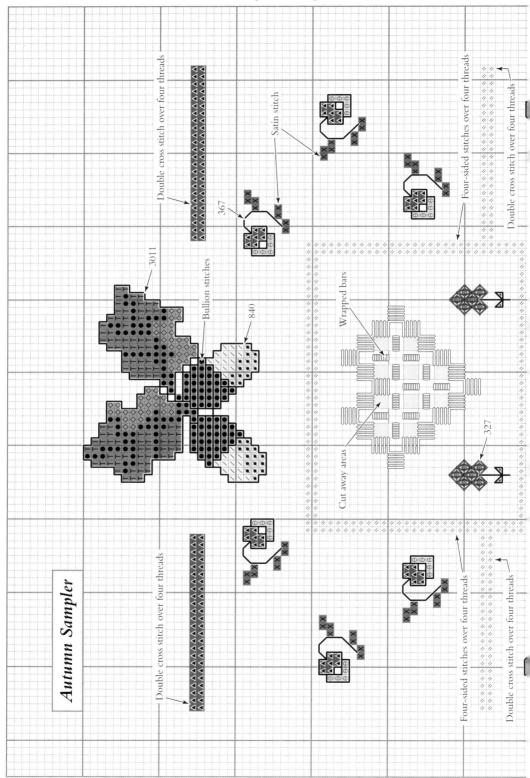

Autumn Sampler

Double cross stitch over four threads

Satin stitch

367

3011

Bullion stitches

840

Wrapped bars

Cut away areas

327

Four-sided stitches over four threads

Double cross stitch over four threads

Double cross stitch over four threads

Four-sided stitches over four threads

Double cross stitch over four threads

French knots
930 and 327
(tweeded)

367

Rice stitch in 729

Half Rhodes stitch
with bar in 729

Queen stitch in 920

Queen stitch in 729

Queen stitch over four threads in 976

Wrapped bars

Wrapped bars

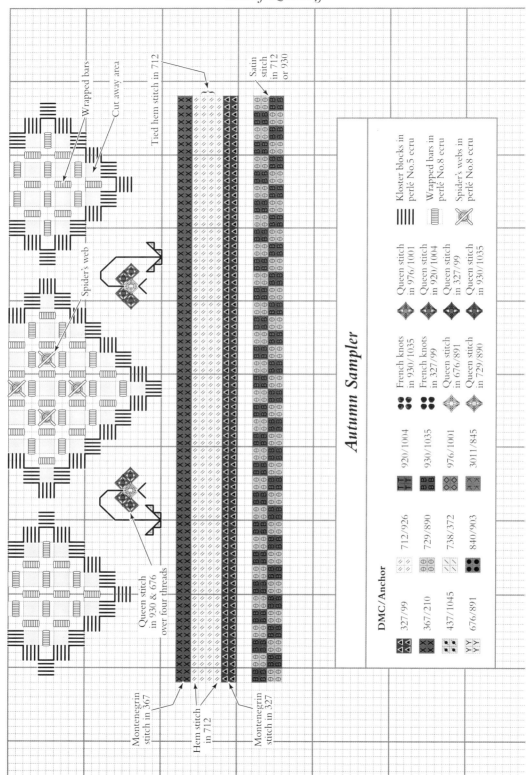

Autumn Sampler

Wrapped bars

Cut away area

Tied hem stitch in 712

Satin stitch in 712 or 930

Spider's web

Queen stitch in 930 & 676 over four threads

Montenegrin stitch in 367

Hem stitch in 712

Montenegrin stitch in 327

		Kloster blocks in perlé No.5 ecru
		Wrapped bars in perlé No.8 ecru
		Spider's webs in perlé No.8 ecru

	Queen stitch in 976/1001
	Queen stitch in 920/1004
	Queen stitch in 327/99
	Queen stitch in 930/1035

	French knots in 930/1035
	French knots in 327/99
	Queen stitch in 676/891
	Queen stitch in 729/890

DMC/Anchor

327/99	712/926	920/1004	
367/210	729/890	930/1035	
437/1045	738/372	976/1001	
676/891	840/903	3011/845	

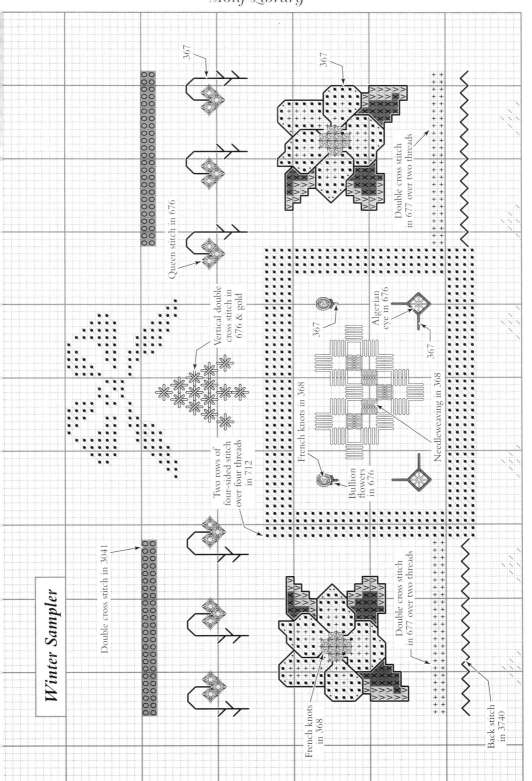

Winter Sampler

Double cross stitch in 3041

367

Queen stitch in 676

Vertical double cross stitch in 676 & gold

Two rows of four-sided stitch over four threads in 712

French knots in 368

Double cross stitch in 677 over two threads

367

Double cross stitch in 677 over two threads

Algerian eye in 676

367

French knots in 368

Needleweaving in 368

Bullion flowers in 676

367

Back stitch in 3740

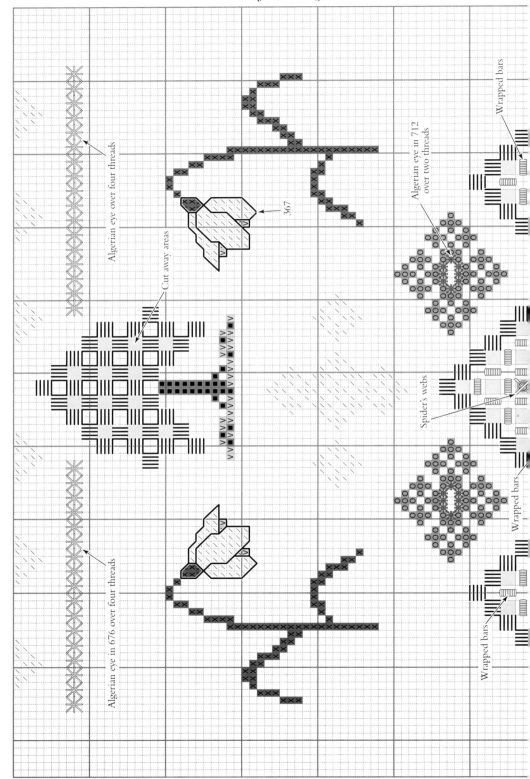

Algerian eye over four threads

Cut away areas

367

Algerian eye in 676 over four threads

Algerian eye in 712 over two threads

Wrapped bars

Spider's webs

Wrapped bars

Wrapped bars

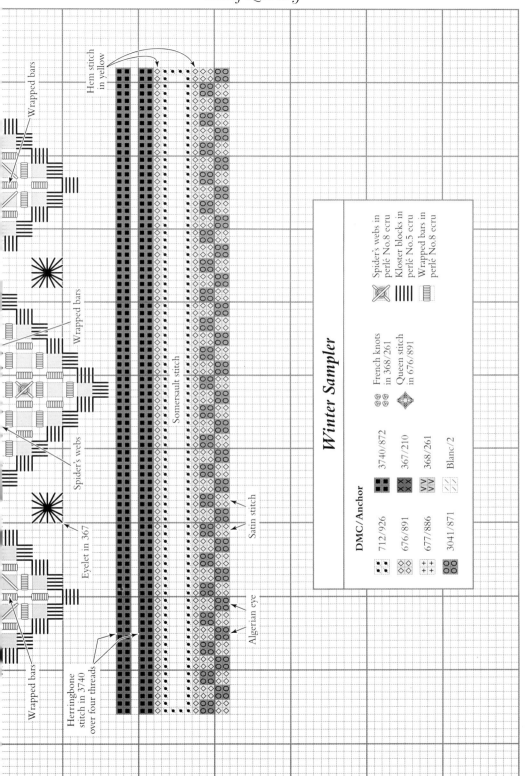

Winter Sampler

DMC/Anchor

712/926		3740/872		French knots in 368/261
676/891		367/210		Queen stitch in 676/891
677/886		368/261		
3041/871		Blanc/2		

Spider's webs in perlé No.8 ecru
Kloster blocks in perlé No.5 ecru
Wrapped bars in perlé No.8 ecru

Wrapped bars

Hem stitch in yellow

Wrapped bars

Somersault stitch

Spider's webs

Satin stitch

Eyelet in 367

Algerian eye

Wrapped bars

Herringbone stitch in 3740 over four threads

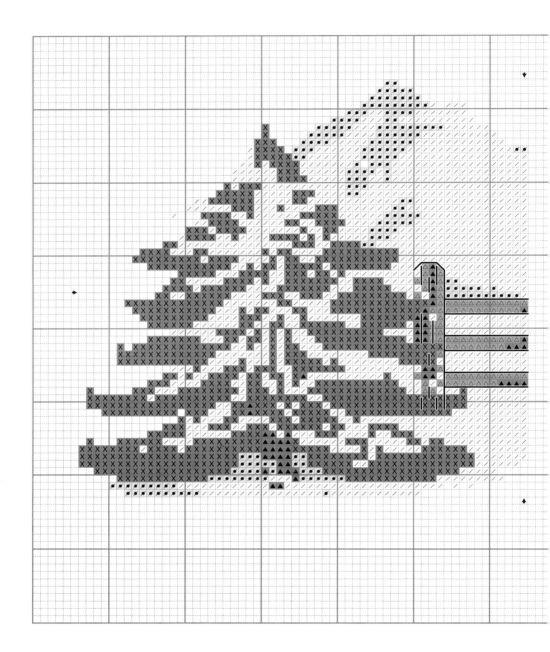

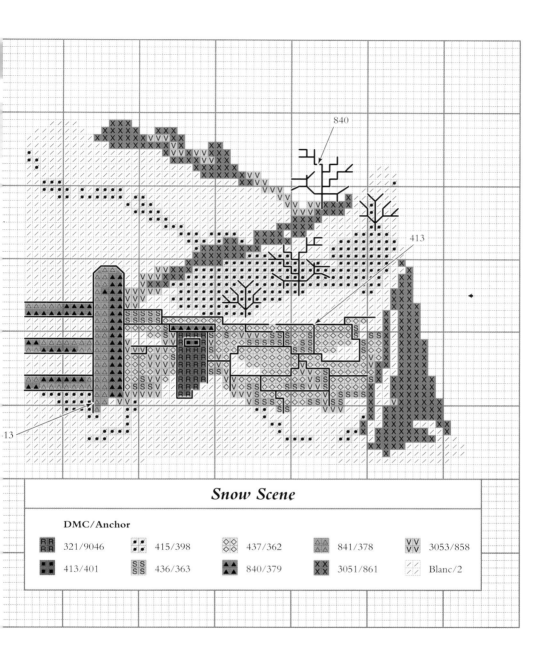

840

413

13

Snow Scene

DMC/Anchor

RR RR 321/9046	415/398	◇◇ 437/362	△△ 841/378	V V V V 3053/858
413/401	SS SS 436/363	▲▲ 840/379	XX XX 3051/861	Blanc/2

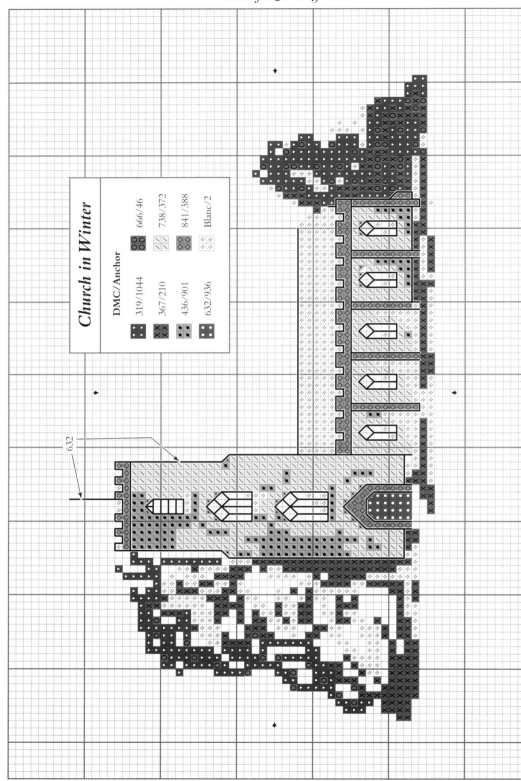

Church in Winter

DMC/Anchor

319/1044	666/46
367/210	738/372
436/901	841/388
632/936	Blanc/2

632

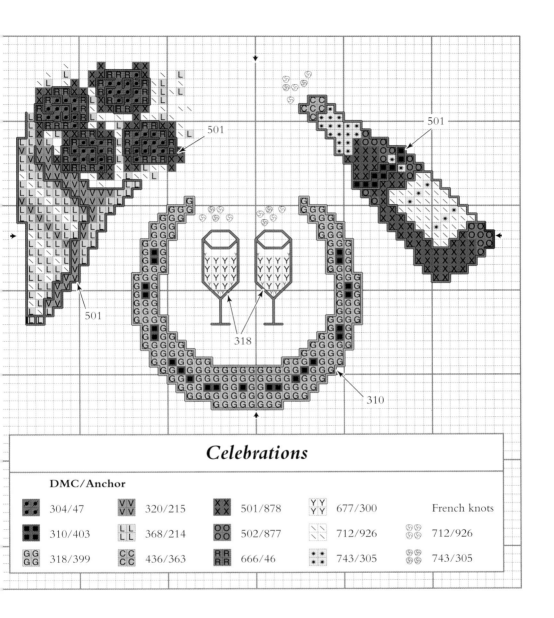

Celebrations

DMC/Anchor

304/47	320/215	501/878	677/300	French knots
310/403	368/214	502/877	712/926	712/926
318/399	436/363	666/46	743/305	743/305

Finishing Techniques

Embroidery designs can be made up into a wonderful range of objects, both practical and decorative and how they are made up or completed makes a great deal of difference to the look of the finished piece. This section describes some of the basic finishing techniques used in the book and suggests ways of displaying your embroidery.

If you are unable to find any items mentioned – don't panic! – there are always alternatives on the market. Experiment!

Washing and Ironing Your Work

If it becomes necessary to wash your embroidery, hand wash the stitching in bleach-free soap, rinse well and remove excess water by squeezing gently in a soft, clean towel. Dry naturally.

To iron a piece of embroidery, first cover the ironing board with four layers of bath towel and press the work from the wrong side using the steam button if your iron has one. Take extra care when ironing work containing buttons and charms and avoid ironing metallic threads.

Stretching and Mounting

Professional framing can be very expensive, but we all feel that our larger projects deserve the professional touch. It is a great shame when after spending hundreds of hours stitching a precious piece of cross stitch, the finished piece is just poked in an unsuitable frame without any further attention. By following the method explained below for padded mounting, you will be able to produce a very good result and have the pleasure of knowing that you completed the whole project on your own. The advantage of a padded mounting for embroidery is that any slightly 'lumpy bits' on the back of your work will be pushed into the padding rather than appear as raised areas on the front of the embroidery.

● Take time to make sure that you have centred the work carefully and that the edges are really straight, otherwise it will show when you put the completed piece in the frame.
● Pad all your completed pieces, even cards, as the padding raises the embroidery, which displays it to better effect.
● Use foamcore board which consists of two layers of thin card with a layer of polystyrene between. This construction makes it easy to cut the board and to pin into the edge as the pins are actually inserted into the polystyrene. You will probably have to buy foamcore board at an artists' supply shop rather than a needlework shop.

You Will Need
3mm foamcore board, or acid-free mounting board
Double-sided adhesive tape, or strong thread for lacing
Polyester wadding (batting) for padding
Glass- or plastic-headed pins

1 Using a sharp craft knife, cut a piece of foamcore to fit your frame (cut round the piece of glass that fits the frame).

2 Attach a piece of wadding (batting) to the foamcore board using two or three strips of double-sided adhesive tape, then trim the wadding to exactly the same size as the foamcore.

3 Position your embroidery on top of the padding and centre it carefully in relation to the padded board. Fix the embroidery in position by pinning through the fabric into the edges of the foamcore board. Start in the middle of each side and pin towards the corners. Make sure your pins follow a line of Aida holes or a thread of linen so that your edges will be really straight. Adjust the fabric's position until you are completely confident that it is centred and straight.

4 Turn the work over, leaving the pins in place, trim the excess fabric to about 5cm (2in) all round and fold it to the back.

pins   cross stitch

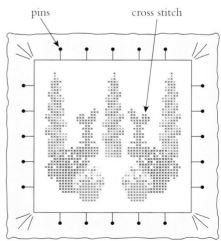

Pining out the embroidery

5 Fix the edges of fabric in place using either double-sided adhesive tape or by lacing across the back using strong thread (see diagram). As the pins remain in place, it is still possible at this stage to adjust the position of the fabric and replace the tape or tighten the lacing. When you are completely satisfied with the result, remove the pins and assemble the frame.

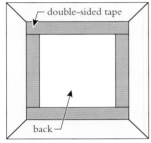

The taping method

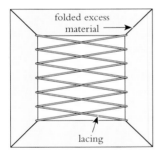

The lacing method

Stretching and Starching Canvas Work

It is the nature of canvas work to distort especially when worked in tent stitch, so it is necessary to stretch and starch the needlework. You will be able to use the board and squared paper many times and will soon master the technique.

You Will Need

A flat, clean board (e.g. chipboard)
Squared paper (e.g. dressmaker's graph paper)
Nails 2.5cm (1in) long
Hammer
Cold water starch (e.g. wallpaper paste without preservatives or anti-fungal agent)
Masking tape
Kitchen palette knife

1 Cover the board with the squared paper and stick down with masking tape.

2 Place the embroidery right side down on the paper. You should be able to see the squares on the paper through the unstitched canvas. Start at one corner and begin nailing down the canvas about 5cm (2in) from the embroidery, hammering in the nails far enough to hold the fabric firmly. Following the line in the canvas, align the canvas with the squared paper, placing nails about 2.5cm (1in) apart (any further apart and the needlework may acquire a scalloped edge). When you have completed the first side, go back to the corner and repeat for the side at right angles to it. In order to square the work, draw a pencil line on the canvas from the first nail you inserted, to the diagonally opposite corner. Work out where this line should end in relation to the lines on the graph paper. Pull the embroidery to this point and nail this corner and then complete the nailing of the last two sides. If your stitching is very distorted it may help to dampen the embroidery.

3 When the last nail is in position the work should be completely square. Mix a small quantity of the starch to the consistency of soft butter and spread it evenly but sparingly with a knife over the canvas, avoiding the unstitched areas. Allow this to dry completely and then remove the nails to remove the work from the board. Not only will the work be completely square but the starch will have evened the tension so your stitches should look even better!

Framing

Needlework generally looks better framed without glass. If you prefer to use glass with this method, you must ensure that the embroidery does not touch the underside of the glass. Insert very narrow strips of board (spacers) into the edges of the frame, between the glass and the mounted embroidery to hold them apart, before you assemble the frame. Always check that both sides of the glass are completely clean. Before adding the final backing board to the back of the picture, line the back of the work with aluminium tin foil to discourage small insects.

When the frame is assembled, seal the back using gummed paper tape, gently pushing the tape into the rebate. The tape will shrink slightly as it dries thus sealing the picture.

Noahs Ark (see page 53) – finished with a frame

Painting Frames and Mounts

When choosing a frame for a particular project, select the largest moulding you can afford and do not worry if the colour is not suitable. Ask the framer to make up the frame and a coloured or gold slip for you, but buy the frame, glass and so on in kit form (most framers do not mind!) and then decorate the frame yourself.

You can use readily available products for this, for example car spray paint (available from car repair or body shop suppliers). There are hundreds of colours in the range, but if you have no luck, try bicycle paints which include even more colours! For subtle matt shades, explore endless possibilities with emulsion paints from DIY shops, often available in tiny tester sizes, ideal for trial and error.

Before you begin to paint a piece of moulding, take care to cover all nearby surfaces with paper or dust cloths, If the moulding is completely untreated, rub down gently with fine sand paper, clean with white spirit on a soft cloth and allow to dry completely before painting.

Making a Bag

A bag or sachet is easy to stitch, can be made in any size and has many different uses – holding small gifts, pot-pourri or wedding mementoes. A bag could be made entirely from Aida or an evenweave fabric, with the design embroidered directly onto the fabric, or it could be made from an ordinary dressmaking fabric with an embroidered panel sewn on. The instructions which follow are for a bag made with stitching fabric with an embroidery design worked on to the fabric. You will need sufficient fabric for the front and back of the bag and a piece of cord or ribbon for a tie.

1 Cut out two rectangles of fabric according to the size you wish your bag to be, and allowing 4cm (1^1/2in) seam allowance all round. Stitch your embroidery design onto the front piece and the back too if you wish.

2 With right sides of the bag rectangles together, pin and stitch both sides and the bottom of the bag, matching the edges for a neat finish. Press the side seams open.

3 To make the top of the bag, fold the top edge over to the wrong side by 6mm (^{1}/4in), press, then fold over again. Pin in place and sew two rows of stitching around the top to form a casing. Turn the bag to the right side. Snip the side seam between the lines of parallel stitching, binding the cut edges with small buttonhole stitches or over-stitching.

4 To finish the bag with a tie, thread a piece of cord or ribbon through the channel and knots the ends to secure.

Making a Band

Stitching a border or a selection of motifs on a band is a lovely way of embellishing all sorts of objects, such as cakes, hats, tie-backs and flower pots. There are many ready-prepared bands available in various widths and with different coloured edgings, or you could cut a length of Aida or linen and hem the edges.

1 Measure the length or circumference of the object to be decorated with the band. Stitch the length of border or row of motifs required, from the centre of the band outwards. When the embroidery is finished, stitch side seams to neaten the ends of the band. If you are using a length of Aida or linen, you will need to stitch seams along the lengths of the band.

2 Sew on pieces of Velcro for fastening the ends or stitch the band to the item being decorated.

Making a Bell Pull

A bell pull is another useful way of displaying cross stitch. You could use one of the designs charted in the Motif Library or design one of your own. A simple rectangular bell pull shape is the easiest to make up but you could make one with a pointed bottom end if you prefer. First, decide on the size of your bell pull – the length of the bell pull hanging rod determines the width of the fabric you need, so buy the bell pull ends and rods before you start stitching. You will also need cotton backing fabric and decorative braid.

1 Work your cross stitch design onto your stitching fabric.

2 Turn under the edges of your evenweave fabric so that your design is central. Fold your backing fabric to the same size and press the turnings.

3 Place the embroidered piece and the backing fabric wrong sides together and pin. Slide the rods in position top and bottom, and add the bell pull ends, then slipstitch the fabric pieces together, adding decorative braid around the edges if desired.

Making a Bookmark

Bookmarks make quick and useful gifts. You could make one of your own (described below) or mount your work in one of the commercially made bookmarks available.

1 Decide on the size of your bookmark and stitch your design onto the fabric.

2 Trim the fabric to within 1cm (^{1}/2in) of the stitching all round. Hem all the sides. If you want to create a shaped point at the bottom, don't hem the bottom but turn it under by about 6mm (^{1}/4in) and tack (baste) (make sure none of the embroidery is included). Find the seam centre point and bring the two corners together so they meet at the back then slipstitch these two edges together. A tassel at the point would finish the bookmark off nicely.

Mounting Work in Cards and Gift Tags

There are many, many blank cards and gift tags available from needlecraft shops and mail-order suppliers. The following method describes mounting work in a card and should be applicable to tags too.

1 When your piece of stitching is complete, press the design on the wrong side and set aside.

2 Open the folded card completely and check that the design fits in the opening. Apply a thin coat of adhesive or double-sided adhesive tape to the inside of the opening (see diagram below). Add the design, carefully checking the position of the stitching before pressing down firmly.

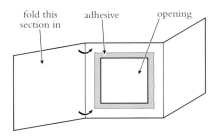

Mounting work into a card

3 Fold the spare flap inside and stick in place with either double-sided adhesive tape or another thin application of adhesive. Leave to dry before closing. Add ribbon trims as desired.

Mounting Work into Commercial Products

There are many items available today which have been specially designed to display embroidery such as trays, stools, fire screens, mugs, boxes, mirrors, trinket pots and coasters.

To mount work in these products, you generally only need to follow the manufacturer's instructions, but it helps to back the embroidered work using iron-on interfacing as this strengthens the stitches and prevents fraying. Interfacing is available from needlework supplies shops and good craft shops. Cut a piece of interfacing a little larger than your stitched fabric, set the iron to a medium heat, or as indicated on the interface instructions, and iron it onto the reverse side of the stitching. Trim the fabric to size before mounting.

Making Cushions, Pincushions and Scissors Keepers

Your cross stitch embroidery can be made up into cushions, pincushions and scissors keepers following the same principles. Basically, two pieces of fabric the same size and shape are joined together, with stuffing inserted into the centre. The fabric may be embroidered on one side or both. There are two main ways of joining the fabrics, using counted chain stitch or normal hand or machine sewing.

To join using counted chain stitch (or long-legged cross stitch), the two fabric sections are joined wrong sides together using counted chain stitch (see page 103) and the stuffing is inserted through an opening before the last side is completed. If a cord for scissors or to attach to a chatelaine is required, insert this immediately after stuffing and anchor it in place as the last side is stitched.

To join using normal hand or machine sewing, proceed as follows. Pin the back and front pieces together, right sides facing (A).

Stitch the pieces together, by hand or machine, leaving an opening to fill with polyester filling (B).

Turn right sides out, insert the filling and slip stitch the opening to close. Make a twisted cord as described on page 187 and slip stitch to the seam, using matching thread and making a join at the bottom and tucking the raw edges inside. Alternatively, you could use a ready-made cord for an edging.

Making a Tassel

Tassels are useful for adding a finishing touch to many projects, including cushions, cards and bookmarks. Tassels can be made from various threads, usually from stranded cottons (floss) to match the cross stitch design, but you could also use metallic threads or tapestry wools.

Decide on the length of tassel you require and cut a square piece of stiff card to this size. Wrap the thread round and round the card (A) to form the body of the tassel, in whatever thickness you require.

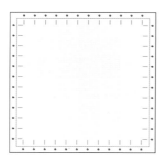

A *Pin front and back together*

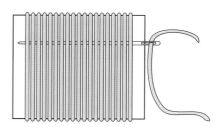

A *Wrap thread around card*

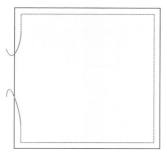

B *Stitch around cushion*

B *Cut bottom threads*

Whilst holding tightly to the top of the tassel, cut across the threads at the bottom and take the tassel off the card (B). Pinch the threads together at the top and tightly wrap a length of thread just below the loop at the top (C). Knot this and thread the ends through to join the other lengths. Trim the tassel ends if they are uneven. To attach the finished tassel, use a length of matching thread through the loop at the top.

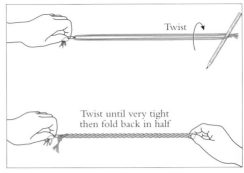

C *Knot the neck*

Making a Twisted Cord

A twisted cord is perfect for finishing off or embellishing many projects. Choose a colour or group of colours in stranded cottons (floss) to match the stitching. Cut a minimum of four lengths, at least four times the finished length required and fold in half. Ask a friend to hold the two ends whilst you slip a pencil through the loop at the other end. Twist the pencil and continue twisting until kinks appear. Walk slowly towards your partner and the cord will twist. Smooth out the kinks from the looped end and tie another knot at the other end to secure.

Bibliography

DE DILLMONT Therese,
Encyclopedia of Needlework (DMC)

EMBROIDERERS' GUILD,
Making Samplers (David & Charles, 1993)

LOVE Janice, *Basics and Beyond*
(Love 'n' Stitches, 1992)

O'STEEN Darlene, *The Proper Stitch*
(Just Cross Stitch, 1994)

SEBBA Anna, *Samplers* (Weidenfield &
Nicholson, 1979)

*The Anchor Book of Hardanger
Embroidery* (David & Charles, 1997)

*The Anchor Book of Ribbon
Embroidery* (David & Charles, 1997)

*The Anchor Book of Counted Thread
Embroidery Stitches* (David & Charles, 1987)

Acknowledgements

A special thank you to my husband Bill and my two special children, James and Louise who have put up with this for the last time!

To Michel Standley, our administrator, who makes it possible for the business to continue whilst I write books; my secretary, Helen King, who writes my lists and makes me follow them, and Sharon Reynolds our housekeeper, who makes it all possible!

A special thanks to all my stitchers, pattern checkers and testers: Hanne Fentiman, Sue Moir, Barbara Webster, Jill Vaughan, Su Maddocks, Glenys Thorne, Michelle Daniels, Susan Bridgens, Ann Sansom, Hanne Lise Stamper, Amanda Lake, Joan Dewar, Violet Holland, Janet Jarvis, Joan Hastewell, Margaret Pallant, Liz Burford, Margaret Locke, Lesley Clegg, Margaret Cornish, Linda Smith, Mary Miles, Doreen Ely, Ann Dudley, Jenny Kirby and Barbara Grenville.

Thanks to all the generous suppliers of the materials and equipment required for this book, particularly Malcolm Turner of Fabric Flair and Rainer Steimann of Zweigart for lovely fabrics, DMC Creative World and Coats Crafts UK for stranded cottons and metallic threads and Ian Lawson Smith for his wonderful I.L.Soft computer programme.

To Cheryl Brown at David & Charles for thinking of me for this title and Linda Clements for editing and sorting out this complicated manuscript. To Brenda Morrison for all her hard work and design flair. To Ethan Danielson for all the excellent technical stitch diagrams and beautiful charts that make this book so special.

Thank you to all the wonderful stitchers who have supported and encouraged me over the past fifteen years and who have made it possible for me to earn a living from my cross stitch passion.

My grateful thanks for help and advice from Mary Jenkins, Brenda Keyes and Moira Blackburn (see Suppliers). Last, but certainly not least, my love and thanks to Sue Hawkins (Technical Director of the Cross Stitch Guild) who has taught me so much and never laughs at my silly questions! This book would not have happened without her.

Jane Greenoff's Inglestone Collection

Jane Greenoff's kit company based in England, supplies cross stitch kits, gold-plated needles, stitching paper and stitchers' gifts. For more information, web site address or Jane Greenoff's classes write to: The Inglestone Collection, Yells Yard, Fairford, Gloucestershire GL7 4BS. Tel: 00 44 1285 712778. Fax: 00 44 1285 713799. E-mail: greenoff@easynet.co.uk

Suppliers

Moira Blackburn
PJA Crafts, 96 Denbrook Avenue, Bradford
BD4 0QN
Cross stitch kits

Coats Crafts UK
PO Box 22, Lingfield, McMullen Road,
Darlington, Co. Durham DL1 1YQ.
Tel: 01325 394394
E-mail: coats.crafts@coats.com
*Stranded cottons and Kreinik blending
filaments, Glow in the Dark and Fine braids*

Daylight Studios,
89–91 Scrubs Lane, London, NW10 6QU.
Tel: 0208 964 1200
Daylight bulbs and lamps

DMC Creative World,
Pullman Road, Wigston, Leicester, LE18 2DY.
Tel: 0116281 1040
Stranded cottons and perlé thread

Fabric Flair (and Beadesign)
Northlands Industrial Estate,
Copheap Lane, Warminster, Wiltshire
BA12 0BG. Tel: 01985 846400
E-mail: mail@fabricflair.com
*Beads and charms, linens and other evenweaves,
Zweigart products, blunt beading needles*

Framecraft Miniatures Ltd,
372 Summer Lane, Hockley, Birmingham,
B19 3QA.
Tel: 0121 212 0551
E-mail: sales@framecraft
Web-site: framecraft.com
Silk gauze, trinket pots and brooches

Hantex Ltd,
Unit 8–10, Lodge Farm Business Units,
Wolverhampton Road, Castlethorpe, Milton
Keynes MK19 7ES. Tel: 01908 511331
E-mail: sales@hantex.co.uk
Novelty buttons and charms

Sue Hawkins (Technical Director of the
Cross Stitch Guild, designer and David &
Charles author)
Needleworks
The Old School House, 67 Hall Road,
Leckhampton, Cheltenham, Gloucestershire
GL53 0HP. Tel: 01242 584424.
E-mail:SueHawkinsNeedleworks@
compuserve.com
Counted cross stitch canvas work and crewel embroidery

Inglestone Collection
Yells Yard, Fairford, Gloucestershire GL7 4AR.
Tel: 01285 712778
E-mail: greenoff@easynet.co.uk
Stitching paper, stitch catchers, gold-plated needles

Mary Jenkins (designer, author and teacher)
22 Alfreda Road, Whitchurch, Cardiff CF14 2EH

Brenda Keyes (designer and author)
The Sampler Company
Holly Tree House, Lichfield Drive, Prestwich,
Manchester M25 0HX. Tel: 0161 773 0914
Cross stitch kits, charts, motif books, thread organisers

Macleod Craft Marketing,
West Yonderton, Warlock Road, Bridge of
Weir PA11 3SR. Tel: 01505 612618
Caron Collection Threads

Quilt Direct,
11 Iliffe House, Iliffe Avenue, Oadby,
Leicester LE2 5LS. Tel: 0116 271 0033
E-mail: sales@quiltdirect.com
Pure silk ribbon (YLI)

Sewing Basket Card Co.
14 Kensington Industrial Park, Hall Street,
Southport, Merseyside, PR9 0NY.
Tel: 01704 549754
Three-fold cards

Zweigart & Sawitzki,
PO Box 120, D–71043 Sindelfingen,
Germany. Tel: 0049 7031 7955
E-mail: info@zweigart.de
Linen, Aida and all other evenweaves

Index

Index